W9-BXS-200

LANGUAGE AND ART IN THE NAVAJO UNIVERSE

Gary Witherspoon

Ann Arbor   The University of Michigan Press

970.3
N318w
1977

Library of Congress Cataloging in Publication Data

Witherspoon, Gary.
   Language and art in the Navajo universe.

   Bibliography: p.
   Includes index.
   1. Navaho Indians—Philosophy.   2. Navaho
language.   3. Navaho Indians—Art.   4. Indians of
North America—Southwest, New—Philosophy.
5. Indians of North America—Southwest, New—Art.
I. Title.
E99.N3W678   970'.004'97   77-3651
ISBN 0-472-08966-8 pbk.

To Gladys Reichard

Grateful acknowledgment is made to the following for permission to reprint copyrighted material:

KC Publications, for material from *Southwestern Indian Ceremonials,* by Tom Bahti. Copyright © 1970 by KC Publications. Reprinted by permission of KC Publications.

Jim McGrath, for poetry from the Public Broadcasting Service film, "R. C. Gorman," 1976. Reprinted by permission of Jim McGrath.

Mouton Publishers, for material from "The Central Concepts of Navajo World View (I)," by Gary Witherspoon, *Linguistics* 119(1974):41–59, © Mouton Publishers, 1974; "The Central Concepts of Navajo World View (II)," by Gary Witherspoon, *Linguistics* 161(1975):69–88, © Mouton Publishers, 1975. Reprinted by permission of Mouton Publishers, The Hague, The Netherlands.

National Geographic Society, for material from "A First American Views His Land," by N. Scott Momaday, *National Geographic,* July 1976, pp. 13–18. Reprinted by permission of National Geographic Society.

The Peter de Ridder Press, for material from "The Central Concepts of Navajo World View," by Gary Witherspoon, in *Linguistics and Anthropology: In Honor of C. F. Voegelin,* edited by M. Dale Kinkade, Kenneth L. Hale, and Oswald Werner. © Copyright reserved, The Peter de Ridder Press, 1975. Reprinted by permission of the Peter de Ridder Press.

Princeton University Press, for excerpts from *Navaho Religion: A Study of Symbolism,* by Gladys A. Reichard. Bollingen Series XVIII. Copyright © 1950, 1963 by Bollingen Foundation. Reprinted by permission of Princeton University Press.

The Rio Grande Press, Inc., for material quoted from *Navajo Shepherd and Weaver,* by Gladys A. Reichard. Copyright © 1968 by The Rio Grande Press, Inc. Quoted material from Rio Grande Classic edition, courtesy The Rio Grande Press, Inc., Glorieta, New Mexico.

The University of Arizona, for excerpts from *Blessingway,* by Leland C. Wyman. Copyright 1970 by University of Arizona Press. Reprinted by permission of University of Arizona Press, Tucson, Arizona.

The University of Chicago Press, for material from *Navajo Kinship and Marriage,* by Gary Witherspoon. Copyright © 1975 by The University of Chicago. Reprinted by permission of The University of Chicago Press.

West Publishing Co., for excerpts from "Visual Metaphors," by Evelyn Payne Hatcher. American Ethnological Society Monograph 58. Copyright © 1967, 1974 by Evelyn Payne Hatcher. West Publishing Co., St. Paul, Minn., 1974. Reprinted by permission of Evelyn Payne Hatcher and West Publishing Co.

Foreword

Gary Witherspoon's work on the Navajo, which is, in its circumspect way, slowly accumulating to a major oeuvre, is part at once
of a persisting, often besieged but apparently indestructible tradition in anthropological research and of an almost quantum-leap
advancement of that tradition now rather broadly underway. The
tradition—one totemically associated with such names as E. E.
Evans-Pritchard, Ruth Benedict, Marcel Mauss, Paul Radin, and
in the particular case of the Navajo, Gladys Reichard (one of the
most underestimated of all American anthropologists, whose long
overdue recognition as a master ethnographer Witherspoon's
work may at last be bringing about)—is that which sees the task of
the discipline to be the comprehension of the frames of meaning
in which other peoples move and the communication of that comprehension to others. The quantum-leap advancement is the
transformation of this tradition from a largely disconnected series
of brilliant forays by scholars of unusual imaginative powers and
enlarged sensibilities, so many ˉhigh-wire tours de force, into a
sustained sequence of systematic investigations. With the work of
such people as David Schneider, Victor Turner, Louis Dumont,
Mary Douglas, Edmund Leach, Stanley Tambiah, Godfrey Lien-
hardt, Nancy Munn, James Fernandez, and by now a veritable
host of scholars of Witherspoon's own generation, the formative
period seems to be giving way to the florescent. What was once a
program, illustrated by sporadic masterpieces, is becoming an enterprise, crowded with converging inquiries.

There are at least three characteristics of this developing style
of analysis that Witherspoon's work displays with particular force
and clarity: the unfrightened acceptance of human diversity; the
passion for ethnographic circumstantiality; and the view that culture is an imaginative form. His work is exemplary, not only because it forces us to confront some of the sturdier immediacies of
Navajo life, rather than merely retailing some additional facts and

a few more theories about it, but also because it shows what the best of this sort of work is like now: direct, meticulous, and frankly interpretive.

The acceptance of diversity—the fact that some of the differences among men are as real, as profound, and as instructive about our nature as the similarities among them—has been something of a stumbling block to studies such as Witherspoon's, trained with total intensity on the life of a single people. The odd notion that if other peoples can be shown to hold well-worked out, articulate opinions about what things are all about ("right" and "wrong," "truth" and "beauty," and all those other grand nouns with which we try to make out what we are committed to) that differ from one's own, one can no longer reasonably hold one's own, grew into a bugbear called cultural relativism, before which many otherwise strong-minded men and women unaccountably quaked. Various devices to exorcise it—searches for cultural universals grounded in psychology, biology, or the supposed necessities of collective living; statistical correlations among cultural facts designed to establish general regularities; arbitrary constructions of historical stages into one or another of which we could all be crammed—were tried, some of them on a rather large scale and with a certain determination, but without much avail. As all good nursemaids know, bugbears disappear most readily when one simply turns one's back on them; and in Witherspoon's work, as that of most recent studies of this sort, the dedication to what Marc Bloch called "the thrill of learning singular things" is quite unapologetic. The Navajos described by Witherspoon are not tokens of anybody's types, not even (except at certain moments when his forgivable romanticism or his even more forgivable exasperation with his own culture's stupidities gets the better of him) his own. They don't represent, stand for, or demonstrate anything but themselves. If one is going to learn anything from them (and anyone who can't learn something from a people who have a "first laugh rite" probably can't learn anything from anybody), it is as that. Only those who confuse the significant with the abstract or like their truths familiar will be discomposed.

The circumstantiality of Witherspoon's work, his unwillingness to be satisfied with the airy generalities that mar some of the lesser works in this tradition, as well as some of the pioneering ones, is apparent on every page. He doesn't just talk about "static" and "active" as vague master ideas, somehow infusing everyone and everything with their spirit; he traces out what such terms come to in the smallest and most concrete details of Navajo language, Navajo classificatory schemes, Navajo ethics, and on into the very patterns they weave into their blankets. When a key term, such as *hózhó*, is explicated, we are not offered easy glosses or strained analogies to Western concepts, but texts and contexts, dozens of them, patiently brought into conjunction with one another until the sense of the term, as the Navajos conceive it, slowly begins to dawn on us, and with it the overall conception of the world in which it is implicated. The extraordinary chapter on subject-object inversion in Navajo speech is one of the very few attempts in the entire literature not just to pronounce that formal considerations independent of cultural understandings are insufficient to an adequate grammatical analysis but to demonstrate the fact in linguistically specific terms. All this makes for more demanding reading than the broad summarizations, seasoned with anecdotes and argued with metaphors, of so many anthropological studies of "ethos and world view." One cannot skim here. But one gets, in the end, more than a general, overall impression of "what Navajos are like." One gets an exact, focused description of particular dimensions of their existence. The difference between a first-rate scholar and one not quite first-rate, Solzhenitsyn remarks in *The First Circle,* is his willingness to "go the final inch." He was talking about mathematicians; but, as the high finicalness of Witherspoon's work shows, it is no less true of ethnographers.

As for the imaginative nature of culture and the interpretive approach to understanding it, it is, with the Navajo, the true subject of the book. At some points—in the discussion of the influence of sandpainting on Jackson Pollock or the shrewd comments on separating the literal from the metaphorical in other cultures—it comes directly to the fore. Most of the time, however, it simply forms the general frame of analysis, coloring everything that is said. Whether it be in unpacking that dense collocation of meanings—Earth Woman, human mothers, the sheep herd, corn field, the mountain soil bundle—designated by the word *shimá,* or sorting out the interworked Navajo conceptions of motion, form, and number, Witherspoon approaches his material with the eye of a man seeking to grasp a deep and difficult idea, not that of one trying to describe an exotic object or a curious practice. The effort is to bring Navajo thought within the range of Western discourse, so that we might have some conception of its nature and some appreciation of its power. One can only hope that, despite what they have suffered at our hands, some day some Navajo scholar will bring our thought into their discourse with as much sensitivity, gravity, tact, and taste, and the long strangeness between us will finally begin to end.

CLIFFORD GEERTZ

Acknowledgments

My greatest debt of gratitude for assistance in writing this book is owed to my many intellectual friends among the Navajo. Chief among these are Hastiin Neez, Asdzaan Yazhi, Dagha Lichii, John Honie, John Dick, George and Mike Mitchell, Joe B. Begay, Rita Wheeler, Jack and Flora Nabahe, Ray Brown, and Billy Sam. Their keen thought, articulate speech, and inquisitive minds made this book possible. Although these friends are outstanding intellectuals, they are not exceptional among the Navajo for that reason. As Navajo culture orients the Navajo toward intellectual and aesthetic creativity, so it is Navajo culture itself for which we must ultimately be grateful for the knowledge, understanding, inspiration, and beauty found in their thought and art.

Robert Young, Ken Hale, Paul Platero, Alton Becker, Vern Carroll, Robbins Burling, Roy Rappaport, David McAllester, and David Schneider carefully read this text and generously offered suggestions for corrections and improvements. I am especially thankful to Robert Young, Ken Hale, and Paul Platero for assisting me with the more technical aspects of Navajo language.

The theoretical orientation of this work derives from and reflects stimulating study with Professors Paul Friedrich, Clifford Geertz, and David Schneider while I was a graduate student at the University of Chicago. I am especially indebted to David Schneider for encouraging me to treat Navajo culture as a unique whole, and to analyze it in its own terms rather than alter or reduce it to conform with some outsider's theory of culture or behavior. The result is that Navajo behavior with regard to language and art are explained and interpreted not in terms of some supposed universal theory of language and art but in terms of Navajo theories of language and art. If I have done a decent job of learning and representing Navajo theories, David Schneider's approach gives the reader an opportunity to learn more about the thinking of Navajos and less about the thinking of the author or some other theoretician.

I am also extremely grateful to Clifford Geertz for his kind and generous foreword. His concepts of human nature and the meaningful contexts within which people formulate their thinking, articulate their feelings, and organize their behavior have been very helpful to me. Geertz's orientation toward the anthropological enterprise as expressed in the last paragraph of the introduction played a significant role in keeping me in anthropology. Geertz's statement about the essential vocation of interpretive anthropology was something with which I could identify, and in that light I have written this book and maintained a marginal relationship with anthropology.

The first draft of several of the following chapters was presented to a graduate seminar on language and culture that was held during the fall semester of 1975 at the University of Michigan. Participants included Sue Lundquist, Susan Nelson, Pat Johnson, Pat Moore, Bill Merrill, Mark Hale, Elizabeth Warantz, Emily Gross, Paul Liffman, John Marsh, David Strecker, David Hughes, Karen Shedlowe, Alton Becker, and Aram Yengoyan. Many of their reactions and suggestions, comments and criticisms helped me in the preparation of the final draft of this book.

The analyses and paradigms found in the four sections of chapter 3 were worked out cooperatively with my wife, Nellie. In sections one and three I relied so heavily on her knowledge and thinking that she should be considered a coauthor. Similarly, Glen Peterson of the art department of Yavapai College was extremely helpful with regard to chapter 4. He not only assisted me in locating appropriate examples of Navajo works of art but he also helped in their analysis. He also assisted me in finding relevant literature on the subject.

I am also extremely grateful to the Rackham School of Graduate Studies at The University of Michigan for a faculty fellowship and research grant which enabled me to complete this study and to prepare it for publication. The grant provided research and clerical assistance which Susan Sanford, Susan Nelson, and Gloria Tacheenie so competently performed. I am also thankful to

Karen Shedlowe for her careful and accurate typing of the manuscript and for her editorial assistance.

I am enormously indebted to the many scholars who have studied and written about Navajo language and culture. Although most of the literature on the Navajo is far from accurate and not worth reading, many works are carefully done and reflect the many years the authors spent among the Navajo and their special interest in various aspects of Navajo culture. I am indebted to all the authors whose works are quoted herein. I have relied most heavily on the works of the linguists Harry Hoijer, Ken Hale, Robert Young, and William Morgan and on the ethnographies of David McAllester, Lee Wyman, Father Berard Haile, and Gladys Reichard. These scholars have spent enormous amounts of time with the Navajo and have done their work well.

Finally, more than anything else, this book represents an extension of the work of Gladys Reichard. Gladys Reichard was one of the great ethnographers of the twentieth century, and her intensive and comprehensive studies of Navajo language and culture represent some of the most complete and most perceptive ethnographic writing ever done. She was one of only a very few ethnographers who took the time to learn to speak Navajo and she was the only ethnographer who took the time to learn how to weave. She was obviously fascinated with Navajo culture and got along well with Navajo people. Her writings reflect the sincerity of her interest, the keenness of her perception, and the warmth of her feelings. Because she did her work so well and because I have benefited from it so much, I have decided to dedicate this work to her honor and memory.

The epigraph and postscript are from Jim McGrath's poetry quoted in the Public Broadcasting Service film, "R. C. Gorman," 1976, and are reprinted by permission of Jim McGrath.

Contents

Illustrations

I can not find enough rainbow ways to travel upon—
I am Navajo:
a person traveling the rainbow,
I am as durable as desert seeds.
I am clear as children's laughter.
I am paradoxical as coyote.
I am as easy to unravel as sage and cochineal blankets.
I am as moving as the swirling log clouds.

—JIM MCGRATH

Introduction

Since the first contact between Europeans and Native Americans, their relationship has been characterized by various forms of estrangement. Attempts by Europeans to overcome this can be seen in their persistent efforts to save the Indians' souls and to improve their way of life. Less compassionate and more self-interested Europeans have been unwilling or uninterested in bridging this gap. Instead, they seem to have dealt with the problem of estrangement by eradicating its source—the Native Americans themselves and their distinctive ways of living. Unfortunately for us all, this latter response has been most frequent and has often been effective. Nevertheless, despite four centuries of European efforts either to exterminate Native Americans or to westernize them, many tribes have survived and many of their unique customs have persisted.

Recently, many white Americans of European descent have become discontented with their own lives and have turned to Native Americans for insight and inspiration. However, instead of taking the time to learn what Native American cultures have to offer, most of these whites have created a mythical super-Indian according to their own fantasies. A product of the white man's disabilities, discontentment, and disillusionment, this twentieth-century "noble savage" has been seen as everything from a militant revolutionary to an impeccable symbol of benevolence and nonviolence, from an all-knowing and all-wise philosopher to a simple child of nature. Although motivated by kindness and sympathy, these latest efforts to applaud and adulate Native Americans tell us more about the fantasies and disabilities of the white man and his culture than they tell us about Native Americans. Accordingly, whites do little to resolve this estrangement and probably contribute additional barriers to its resolution, for the creation of a mythical super-Indian obscures our vision of specific Indians and their basic humanity.

This book is written with an optimistic and hopeful attitude. I believe that many Indians and non-Indians would like to bridge the gaps of misunderstanding which separate them while reaping some of the rewards of human communion that result when racial, linguistic, and cultural barriers are overcome. Building such bridges is an extensive and difficult task, and this book is just one relatively small aspect of that task. Nevertheless, I sincerely hope it is a contribution, however small, to that endeavor.

When we leave our comfortable surroundings of familiar things and people, understandable behavior and speech, interpretable events and manageable gadgets and move into the world of another people, we are immediately confronted with streams of strange speech and behavior, confounded further by their appearance in an unfamiliar context of foreign things, faces, and places. Our first perception of these strange faces and places tends to be dominated by a feeling or conception of their uniformity. As a result, superficial acquaintance with one Native American culture leads us to draw inaccurate conclusions about all of them. Further observation, however, allows us to see their great diversity.

Intensive and extensive acquaintance with the variety of Native American cultures may eventually lead us to a better understanding of actual commonalities and regularities among them. Nevertheless, for now, it seems to me to be necessary to occupy ourselves with attempts to understand particular cultures better. However, if we attempt to understand everything at once, we will wind up understanding nothing very well; therefore, this book is focused not just on one particular culture but on specific, though very significant, aspects of that culture. The focus here is on the role and nature of language and art in Navajo life and culture.

Clifford Geertz claims that "the aim of anthropology is the enlargement of the universe of human discourse" (1973:14). Human discourse is a broad and extensive phenomenon, involving many channels and vehicles through which messages are transmitted and interpreted. Language is, of course, one of the more important vehicles of discourse, but it is not by any means the only one. Nor is discourse necessarily the only important function of language.

Language is, among other things, a symbolic code by which messages are transmitted and understood, by which information is encoded and classified, and through which events are announced and interpreted. When we hear an unfamiliar language spoken, it is obvious to us that we cannot understand what is being said. Like speech, human actions are also performed within and according to a particular symbolic code and the meanings of such actions are not always apparent. These actions, whether dressing in a certain way, behaving in a certain way, or eating a particular kind of food in a special way, all convey messages about the thoughts, feelings, and beliefs of the persons who perform them.

Whereas we have little basis for jumping to conclusions about the meanings of foreign sounds that are part of a foreign language, we do have a persistent and pervasive propensity to jump to conclusions about the meanings of foreign acts. We have a tendency to take behaviors at face value, regardless of the cultural context within which they take place. Deeper involvement in the cultures of other people, however, leads us to the recognition that the meanings of their acts are not as apparent or transparent as we might initially have thought them to be. In fact, we find that our initial interpretations of their actions were made according to a symbolic code that we brought to their world from our world, and that correct interpretations of their actions have to be made according to their symbolic code.

Like language, culture is a symbolic code through which messages are transmitted and interpreted. But, more than a code, culture is a set of conceptions of and orientations to the world, embodied in symbols and symbolic forms. Through the adoption of and adherence to particular concepts of and orientations to reality, human beings actually create the worlds within which they live, think, speak, and act. This is what Berger and Luckmann (1966) have called the process of world construction, or the social construction of reality. Although all human beings apparently occupy the same globe, they traverse very different worlds. These worlds vary in their style of construction, in their operation and maintenance, in the entities that fill, decorate, and obstruct them, and in the categories and classes to which these entities are assigned. Thus the basis of a particular cultural code is an ideological system by which the world is defined, described, and understood.

The behavior and institutions of another people must be viewed, at least initially, against the backdrop of their view of the world or their ideological frame of reference. Their conception of the nature of reality, its operation and constitution, shapes their value orientations, behavioral codes, and classificatory structures, all of which are surface level phenomena (or initial subsurface level, depending on one's perspective). Brief acquaintance with these surface level phenomena of another culture leads one to view a people's thought as more rational and their behavior as more sensible. But more careful observation and analysis leaves us with a great deal of confusion, paradox, and ambiguity. The problem is that surface level phenomena need to be understood and explicated in subsurface level terms to be most accurately comprehended.

Just as the surface structure of a given sentence is generated by a set of operations at the deep structural level, concepts of and orientations to the world (that which is described in a world view portrait) emanate from deeper level metaphysical assumptions. All conceptual schemes have to start with one or more assumptions from which the whole scheme is ultimately derived. All things that make a people's customs rational and sensible to them and intelligible to others are founded on these primary metaphysical assumptions.

It ought to be obvious that a set of phenomena do not explain or generate themselves. One part of a system cannot be adequately explained by reference to other parts on the same level, or to the whole of that system. That is the problem with functionalism, operationalism, and even formalism (Piaget, 1970:32–33). Every conceptual scheme or social system has been derived from more primal assumptions. A kinship system is ultimately based on a theory of reproduction, and theories of reproduction are based on more primal metaphysical assumptions. These more primal assumptions may be based on an even more primal assumptioı Higher level schemes (those closer to the surface and more easily observed or discovered) are explicable in terms of the lower level assumptions from which they are derived. At the bottom of all this explanation is ultimately the unexplainable—the primordial assumption from which the whole world is constructed.

I hesitate to say that lower level assumptions generate higher level ones, as is claimed in generative grammar with regard to surface and deep structures. I prefer the term *derived* because a lower level assumption can be a basis for more than one higher level scheme. In fact the higher the level—that is, the farther one gets from the primordial assumption—the greater chance there is for variance. A particular assumption may serve as the basis for multiple propositions, which once proposed and sanctioned, become assumptions for still further propositions. The more assumptions with which one has to work, the more different kinds of schemes and systems he can create.

It is my hypothesis (because there is little data available on this matter) that all cultures are constructed from and based on a single metaphysical premise which is axiomatic, unexplainable, and unprovable. I do not, however, assume that this metaphysical premise is the same for all cultures, but I do think that it may be the same for many cultures which appear on the surface to be quite different from each other. A single premise can serve as the starting point for more than one conceptual scheme or ideological system. From this single premise a conceptual scheme develops by the positing of an opposition to it, from which it is then expanded into a more complex structure utilizing analogy, opposition, and synthesis as its tools of construction.

By the hypothesis above I do not wish to enter the treadmill of debate concerning independent invention versus diffusion, for both obviously were important factors in the development, growth, and distribution of various cultural forms. But I do wish to argue that apparently major and significant changes can occur on the surface level of a cultural system without alterations to its more fundamental metaphysical assumptions. These surface changes require a process of world remodeling through which they are reconciled with lower level assumptions. Through this process of reconciliation the cultural system returns to an ordered and coherent whole. What I am trying to uncover and articulate in this work is the constant and enduring core of Navajo culture—that which gives Navajo culture its unique and dynamic force and vitality through times of stress and change as well as through times of plenty and prosperity.

Learning the nature, structure, constitution, and operation of another culture is not easy. I have spent the better part of fifteen years now living with Navajos and trying to learn to converse with them. It is a task which often seems to succeed only distantly, but sometimes an insight, like a ray of sunlight, seems to open up new vistas of understanding. These vistas of understanding, imagined or real, provide a basis for further conversations through which they are either corrected or sustained. Insights into another culture do not come from idle contemplation or superficial fieldwork based on questions *about* and observations *of* it; they come from intensive and extensive, serious and humorous, involvement *in* it.

My "fieldwork" among the Navajos has been of a very different nature from the typical anthropological pattern of one- to two-year visits to a strange culture and then a welcomed return to home. I have been a resident-worker-affine in several Navajo communities and have made my home on the reservation for a period extending beyond ten years. I have never been in these communities for the purpose of anthropological research.[1] I was there originally as a nineteen-year-old Mormon missionary and came back as a teacher, community worker, and school administrator. In all of these latter roles I was an employee of the local Navajo community, hired by the local Navajo board of education, and assigned tasks within the structure of their goals and aspirations. I participated in their activities and attended their ceremonies, not as an outside and temporary observer, but as an interested and concerned helper and friend. Thus I never took field notes, never recorded a song or a prayer, never photographed a ceremony or a sandpainting, and never had an interview with an "informant." I learned the culture as an interested and concerned participant, not as a detached observer. What I know about Navajo culture comes from my heart and my head, not from my file cabinet or my field journal. Navajos taught me that anything you cannot remember without writing down is something you do not know or understand well enough to use effectively. So I have tried to learn about Navajo life and culture by entering it, not by recording or inscribing it.

The first and best entry into another culture is through the language. It has been from my attempts to learn Navajo and to converse with Navajos in their language that I have gained a few insights into the structure and operation of their world. Accordingly it seems appropriate to introduce others to the Navajo world by focusing on the role and nature of language in that world. As will be seen in the chapters to follow, it is through language that the world of the Navajo was created, and it is through language that the Navajos control, classify, and beautify their world.

The greatest value of learning the language of another people does not come from being able to interview informants without interpreters or from providing native terms in ethnographic writings; it comes from being able to understand what the natives say and how they say it when they are conversing with each other. I have learned by far most of what I know about the Navajo world by listening to Navajos converse with each other about matters of immediate interest and concern to themselves. By listening to their conversation I learned what matters are important to the Navajos, how they think and talk about such matters, how they explain and analyze them, and how they attempt to deal with them.

Whenever an interviewer initiates a conversation with an informant, he constructs a frame within which his informant must respond. The informant does not simply tell the interviewer what is on his mind, he has to deal with what is on the mind of the ethnologist, and it is, therefore, no wonder that so many informants get bored so easily and fail to show up at appointed times. The universe in which they respond to the ethnologists' questions is an artificial one, and ethnographic reports based solely on questions and responses in this universe are correspondingly superficial.

Another important aspect of my methodology is work with Navajo intellectuals and philosophers. Among the Navajos there are a number of men and women who take a special interest in why things are the way they are and why people behave the way they do. Such people often develop extensive and complex theories and philosophies to explain the events and things they question. Such theories are not only not shared with or known by the general population but usually differ somewhat significantly from each other. These people are the Navajo Aristotles, Freuds, Webers, and Darwins. Just as is true for such people as Jung and Freud, Weber and Marx, Plato and Aristotle, the theories of Navajo intellectuals, however different on the surface, are all found to be based on similar assumptions about the nature and operation of reality.

This is not a book of native theories, although such a book would be of great interest and value in its own right. It is an attempt to articulate the metaphysical assumptions with which Navajos think and according to which they analyze and explain the events that occur in their world. What I have been especially interested in is not the surface level content of theories that Navajo intellectuals have proposed, but the underlying premises according to which those theories are rationally and logically drawn conclusions. In this book I am attempting to uncover and elaborate the generative ideas from which Navajo culture sprang and according to which Navajo thinking has proceeded for an indeterminable number of centuries. These ideas provide the basic metaphysical orientations according to which the Navajo have absorbed many surface level ideas and practices, and by which they have reordered them according to a peculiarly Navajo framework and transformed them according to a peculiarly Navajo style.

An example of the kind of underlying metaphysical premise to which I am making reference would be the Western conception of the relationship between mind and body or mind and matter. Especially since the Cartesian age of natural and mental philoso-

phy, and possibly even before, Western thought has been dominated by the basic and complete separation of mind and matter,
idea and entity, and subject and object. To Western thinkers what
goes on in the mind is subjective, while that which occurs in the
world of matter and energy is objective. According to this premise
about the nature and operation of reality, thought alone has no
impact on the structure and operation of reality, and spoken
words have no power to control matter or energy. These basic
metaphysical notions which are taken for granted by most Western intellectuals are denied in Navajo thought. Navajo philosophy
assumes that mental and physical phenomena are inseparable,
and that thought and speech can have a powerful impact on the
world of matter and energy.

If one assumes a Western metaphysical stance with regard to the
nature of mind and matter, speech and energy, he will never be
able to comprehend how the world can be created and controlled
through language, how a person cannot be mentally keen but
physically lazy, or why a horse cannot kick a man. Navajo interpretations of the constitution of reality and the causation of events are
all based on an unbreakable connection between mind and matter,
speech and event. In this regard, primary importance and creative
power is always attributed to thought and speech. These metaphysical notions will all be discussed in detail later and are simply
mentioned here by way of illustration and introduction.

Another way in which I have tried to unravel and uncover
Navajo metaphysical assumptions is by methods traditionally associated with philology. Fortunately, in the case of the Navajo, there
is an abundance of written accounts of the prayers and songs of
most of the important Navajo rituals, as well as written accounts
of most of the episodes found in Navajo mythology. These
significant literary texts contain and express Navajo assumptions
about the nature and operation of the world, but the meanings
and implications of these expressions are not easily comprehended, and on their surface they are enigmatic. Nevertheless,
when the methods and practices of the philologist are combined
with other methods and the data which they yield, the careful

study of literary texts can be very valuable and provide many insights into the Navajo world.

Finally, in describing my methodology and orientation, I see human behavior as both the beginning and the end of all ethnographic description and analysis. Although behavior does not generate or explain itself, it does provide a key to its own analysis, and is the chief artifact from which that which does explain behavior can be constructed. Constructing or, more properly, reconstructing the intellectual foundations of a culture has its parallel with archaeological analysis. In both cases we work with artifacts— that is, observable data—from which inferences are made about unobservable systems. If correctly inferred, the social/cultural system which the archaeologist infers from his data (artifacts) ultimately turns around and explains or accounts for the data. Moreover, an important but often obscured stimulation for and aim of archaeological work is not so much to explain the past as to explain why certain things (artifacts) exist in the present, and why they exist in the particular place and form in which they are found. In archaeology, artifacts provide the point of departure for all systematic analysis, but they are also the culmination point of all analysis and explanation.

No adequate description or valid analysis of a cultural system can be developed or inferred without reference to human behavior; and the cultural system, if accurately inferred, must ultimately (either by itself or, as I believe, in combination with other factors) explain the behavior from which it is inferred. Nevertheless, just as an isolated artifact treated independently could not yield much information about the social system from which it was derived, human behavior taken alone is a grossly inadequate basis for inferring the cultural system from which it derives. It must be considered in relationship to and in context with other data available to the ethnologist.

The premises of Navajo metaphysics with which I will be dealing in the early chapters of this book are not those which Navajos can easily articulate without extended reflection. They are so axiomatic in the Navajo scheme of things that no Navajo ever gives them any thought. This is probably true of all peoples. Most professional intellectuals, let alone lay people, are not fully aware of or able to articulate the axiomatic premises on which their own thinking is based. Although Navajos do not normally articulate their basic metaphysical assumptions, they can easily determine when someone has them wrong. The responses of Navajos themselves to the statements I make provide one of the best tests for the validity of those statements. Even though one cannot easily articulate the axiomatic assumptions according to which his world is constructed, he can easily tell when they are contradicted.

Ultimately a major test of validity has to be whether and to what extent the account of a people's world adequately explains and makes intelligible the events of that world.

The claim to attention of an ethnographic account does not rest on its author's ability to capture primitive facts in faraway places and carry them home like a mask or a carving, but on the degree to which he is able to clarify what goes on in such places, to reduce the puzzlement—what manner of men are these?—to which unfamiliar acts emerging out of unknown backgrounds naturally give rise. . . . If ethnography is thick description and ethnographers those who are doing the describing, then the determining question for any given example of it . . . is whether it sorts winks from twitches and real winks from mimicked ones. It is not against a body of uninterpreted data, radically thinned descriptions, that we must measure the cogency of our explications, but against the power of the scientific imagination to bring us into touch with the lives of strangers (Geertz, 1973:16).

Whereas the major motivation of this book is to bring the Navajo world closer and make it more intelligible to non-Navajos, another purpose is to illustrate what Navajo thought and art have to offer philosophy and art in general. To the extent I understand them, Navajo views of language and reality, and man's relationship to both, are not presented simply to help us better understand the Navajo; they are also presented to help us better understand language and reality. I believe the Navajo have something significant to contribute to the philosophical study of language and art and to our understanding of the relationship between mental and physical phenomena.

Although the latter motivation for this book, in which Navajo philosophy and art take their place alongside other philosophies and art traditions and in which Navajo intellectuals and artists take their place alongside other intellectuals and artists, is out of line with traditional anthropological ethnographies, it is not out of line with what Geertz views to be the essential vocation of interpretive anthropology:

To look at the symbolic dimensions of social action—art, religion, ideology, science, law, morality, common sense—is not to turn away from the existential dilemmas of life for some empyrean realm of de-emotionalized forms; it is to plunge into the midst of them. The essential vocation of interpretive anthropology is not to answer our deepest questions, but to make available to us answers that others, guarding other sheep in other valleys, have given, and thus to include them in the consultable record of what man has said (1973:30).

CHAPTER 1

Creating the World
through Language

The Navajo term *nahaghá* ("ritual") labels a large and significant
category of Navajo behavior which non-Navajos least understand,
and thus constitutes a major dimension of the estrangement that
divides Navajos and non-Navajos. Navajos possess and perform
over sixty major rites and numerous minor ones. They perform
rituals for blessing, for curing, and for purification. They bless
(make immune to illness and tragedy) their land, their livestock,
their crops, their homes, their property, their relatives, and themselves. They cure both mental and physical disorders, as well as
disorders in their environment. They purify things, places, and
themselves after inadvertent, inastute, or inappropriate contact
with potentially dangerous things. Navajos perform these rites,
not at any set or specified times, but when conditions or circumstances require them.

One occasion when some Navajos felt the need for ritual behavior occurred in 1969 when I was spending the summer at the
home of John Dick. That summer an active woman of eighty-two
years became rather suddenly ill. She was taken to the Project
Hope hospital in Ganado, Arizona. She quickly fell into a coma
and remained in that condition for over two weeks. She was kept
alive at the hospital by intravenous feeding. The family consulted
a diviner who diagnosed her case as being caused by contact with
the ghost of a deceased non-Navajo. The Enemyway rite was the
prescription. Family members then petitioned the doctors at the
hospital to release the woman for the performance of the ritual.
The doctors counseled that once she was off intravenous feeding
she would soon die. Undaunted, the family members brought her
home and quickly began the rite for which they had been prepar-
ing and planning. When she arrived at her home, she seemed to

me to be in a deep coma, totally unconscious, and nearly dead. Before the rite was over (it lasted three days), she regained consciousness and was eating and talking. By the conclusion of the rite she was walking around almost normally. Several non-Navajos working at the local school were amazed; most Navajos were not amazed but were gratefully serene. I last saw her, alive and well, in 1973.

In this short narrative of observable behavior and events—a sort of ethnographic artifact—we have a case of unfamiliar acts emerging out of unknown backgrounds; and, as such, they both demand and, to some extent, defy explanation. But since a tumult of events that lack both interpretation and interpretability tends to unhinge our minds (Geertz, 1966:14), we seek interpretations and explanations of strange behaviors and events.

When non-Navajos are asked why the Navajos in this case (or any other case for that matter) went through the elaborate, expensive, and rigidly established behavior that the Enemyway rite demands, the answer is almost always that they did so because that is what their religion prescribes. Such an explanation casts itself into a category of our world (that is, religion) that does not correspond to anything in the Navajo world. The term *nahaghá* bears no semiotic or syntagmatic relationship to the word 'religion'.

In explaining the ailment and its cure non-Navajos again rely on their own categories of belief and description. They attribute the event either to coincidence or to psychosomatic effect. Coincidence is a statistical hypothesis based on a theory of randomness, for which there is not only no proof but not even an adequate definition (Chaitin, 1975:47–52). Psychosomatic effect is just a label for a set of observed behaviors involving the power of the mind over the body, for which there is no adequate explanation in operational terms. Nevertheless, regardless of their adequacy, these explanations are again cast not in the ideological or ontological frame of the world in which they occurred, but in the ideological and ontological frame from which they were observed. These explanations tell us nothing about the Navajo world, and serve only as barriers to our understanding of it.

More sophisticated and empathetic thinkers may try to find an explanation for these events in the therapeutic value of Navajo rituals. Regardless of whether Navajo rituals have such therapeutic value, such explanations are cast in terms of Western psychology, based on Western ideas of personality, behavior, and mental illness and its cure. Here again we seek to explain events in their world, and thus reduce the estrangement we feel, by finding a parallel or an affinity between our beliefs and their practices. In the process, however, we miss the affinity between their beliefs and their practices, and thus remain oblivious to the initial basis on which our understanding of their behavior must be founded.

Gearing tells us that *"when one is estranged he is unable to relate, because he cannot see enough to relate to"* (1970:4). To relieve or overcome this estrangement, however, one often creates a fetish out of empathy and relates to it. But the escape is an illusion, and the relatedness it establishes is unilateral. Gearing adds that *"the opposite of being estranged is to find a people believable"* (1970:5). This probably goes too far. Estrangement may be overcome by simply discovering the rationality of their thought and the sensibility of their behavior.

Navajo acts arise out of their world and make sense within it. Before we can make sense out of ethnographic dramas, we must know the stages on which they are played, and the scripts according to which they are performed. Navajo dramas take place on Navajo stages, and are acted out according to Navajo scripts. We must know the origin and constitution of both their stage and their scripts, if we are to understand the meaning of their plays. This is especially true if we, like Geertz (1973:5), take the analysis of culture to be not an experimental science in search of law but an interpretative one in search of meaning. Ultimately, however, we must search for universals, but universals cannot correctly be inferred from inadequately understood or inappropriately explained data.

The world in which Navajos live and act was brought into being by the *Diyin Dine'é* ("Gods," "supernaturals," or often, incorrectly, "Holy People").[1] These *Diyin Dine'é* entered the sweathouse and thought the world into existence (Wheelwright, 1942:57–59; Wyman, 1970:115). Their thoughts were realized through speech, song, and prayer. Wheelwright (1942:60) has recorded the "Beginning of the World Song" (my translation of the Navajo text):

First Verse: The earth will be,
                the mountains will be,
                (and so on, mentioning other things to be)

Second Verse: The earth will be, from ancient
                times with me there is knowledge of it.
                The mountains will be, from ancient
                times with me there is knowledge of it.
                (and so on)

Third Verse: The earth will be, from the very
                beginning I have thought it.
                The mountains will be, from the very
                beginning I have thought it.
                (and so on)

Fourth Verse: The earth will be, from ancient times
                I speak it.
                The mountains will be, from ancient times
                I speak it.
                (and so on)

Fifth Verse: (The fifth verse is a repetition of the first
                verse, rendering the sense "and so it will be"
                or "and thus it will be done.")

Wyman records and translates a similar song in Blessingway (1970:113–14):

(1) of Earth's origin I have full knowledge . . .
(2) I had full knowledge from the very beginning . . .
(3) Long ago he was thinking of it . . . of [Earth's] origin
    he was thinking . . .

(4) Long ago he spoke of it . . .
he speaks of [Earth's] origins.

Thinking and singing the world into existence attributes a definite kind of power to thought and song to which most Westerners are not accustomed. It is rather obvious that the Navajo ontological conception of thought and speech is very different from our own. To discover and comprehend this difference it is necessary to look at the origins of thought and speech in Navajo mythology. In the account of the creation of this world found in Blessingway, First Man speaks to two beings who are the apparent personifications of thought and speech:

"Of all these various kinds of holy ones that have been made, you the first one will be (represent) their thought, you will be called Long Life [*Sq'ah Naagháii*]," he was told. "And you who are the second one, of all Holy People that are put to use first, you will be (represent) their speech, you will be called Happiness [*Bik'eh Hózhǫ*]," he was told. That much so happened. "You will be (found) among everything (especially ceremonial affairs) without exception, exactly all will be long life by means of you two, and exactly all will be happiness by means of you two," was said to them (Wyman, 1970:398).

The pair mentioned in the passage above originated out of First Man's medicine bundle. When they arose, they were said to be without equal in their beauty and radiance, each having long hair extending to the thighs. At this time it was said that they would never be seen again, although their existence would be constantly manifested in their capacity to sustain life on the earth (Wyman, 1970:112). These two beings are sometimes referred to as First Boy and First Girl, with thought being male and speech being female. They are considered to be the parents of Changing Woman, the benevolent female deity who is identified with the Earth (Earth Woman being another one of her names) and is the source and sustenance of all life on the earth's surface, controlling particularly fertility and fecundity.

The names of these two beings—*Sa'ah Naagháii*, identified with thought, and *Bik'eh Hózhǫ́*, identified with speech—are used in almost every song and prayer found in the numerous rites of the Navajo. In fact they constitute in linguistic form the ideal world of the Navajo, and they contain most of the important concepts and meanings that pervade the Navajo world. *Hózhǫ́* may be glossed as 'a beautiful, pleasant, and healthy environment'. *Sǫ'ah Naagháii* is that which precedes and produces *hózhǫ́*. *Bik'eh* means 'in accordance with it' or 'by its decree'. Kluckhohn (1949:368–69) identified *hózhǫ́* as the central idea in Navajo religious thinking. But it is not something that occurs only in ritual song and prayer; it is referred to frequently in everyday speech. A Navajo uses this concept to express his happiness, his health, the beauty of his land, and the harmony of his relations with others. It is used in reminding people to be careful and deliberate, and when he says good-bye to someone leaving, he will say *hózhǫ́ǫgo nanináa doo* ("may you walk or go about according to *hózhǫ́*").

Sǫ'ah Naagháii Bik'eh Hózhǫ́ has been translated numerous ways, all of which have been grossly inadequate. The most common of these translations is the one popularized by Father Berard Haile, who describes *sǫ'ah naagháii* as 'long life' and *bik'eh hózhǫ́* as 'happiness'. Other translations include the following: 'in-old-age-walking-the-trail-of-beauty'; 'according-to-age-may-it-be-perfect'; and 'according-to-the-ideal-may-restoration-be-achieved' (Reichard, 1950a:46–47). Robert Young considers *sǫ'ah naagháii* to represent the capacity of all life and living things to achieve "immortality" (perpetuate the species) through reproduction. He feels *bik'eh hózhǫ́* represents the peace and harmony essential to the perpetuation of all living species. He further notes that these perfect prototypes, along with the prototypes of rain and other requisite elements of life, were placed in the Sacred Mountains and function now to make the reproduction and sustenance of all living things possible (Young, personal communication).

After attempting to outline many of the Navajo concepts concerning the nature of man and the world, Reichard concluded:

> Consideration of the nature of the universe, the world, and
> man, and the nature of time and space, creation, growth,
> motion, order, control, and life cycle includes all these and
> other Navajo concepts expressed in terms quite impossible to
> translate into English. The synthesis of all the beliefs de-
> tailed above and of those concerning the attitudes and expe-
> riences of man is expressed by *sa'ą na·yái,* usually followed
> by *bik'e xójó·n* (1950a:45).

Nearly every song and prayer in the elaborate Navajo ceremonial system uses *są'ah naagháii bik'eh hózhǫ́* in its benediction. In
fact, the entire ceremonial system is primarily designed to produce or restore the conditions symbolized by the phrase *są'ah
naagháii bik'eh hózhǫ́.* In an attempt to elaborate further on the
meaning of this phrase, I will proceed to an analysis of the implicit meanings of each lexical item:

Są'ah

The etymology[2] of *są'ah* seems to indicate that this term is a deri-
vative of the past tense form of the verb stem 'to grow, to mature'.
This verb stem is used widely to denote someone or something
that is mature, ripe, experienced, or aged. Father Berard Haile
concluded that *są'ah* refers to old age as a goal in life (Wyman,
1970:29). For the Navajo death of old age is considered to be both
natural and highly desirable.

In Navajo mythology Coyote, the philosopher, argued that death
had to be a part of the scheme of this world. He argued that if
death did not occur, the earth would soon be overcrowded, and
there would be no room for corn fields. He concluded that it was
better for each person to live a limited time and then leave and
make room for the children. The people recognized the wisdom of
his words and agreed that it would be so (Reichard, 1950a:42).

Birth and death are recognized as structural opposites; one cannot exist without the other. This is manifested in mythology when Monster Slayer, who is in the process of killing the enemies of the people, comes upon Old Age with the intention of killing him:

Directly Old Age also spoke up, "In spite of all, I am going to live on, my grandchild," he said. . . . "You have not the right thing in mind, I see," he told him. "Should you kill me dying would cease," he said. "Then too giving birth would cease," he said, "and this present number of people would continue in the same amount for all time to come. While if I live on, old age will do killing and giving birth will go on in the future. As giving birth goes ahead, so deaths will go on the other way," he said. "The various birth beings, all without exception, should continue to give birth in the future, every kind of moving being, none excepted," he said. "Now think this over, my grandchild, you can see now how this thing is!" he told him (Wyman, 1970:573).

Life is considered to be a cycle which reaches its natural conclusion in death of old age, and is renewed in each birth. Death before old age is considered to be unnatural and tragic, preventing the natural completion of the life cycle. Whereas illness usually comes from various forms of disorder and disharmony, premature death usually results from malevolent intentions and deeds. Ceremonies, however, have been provided by the Holy People to combat the suffering and misfortune caused by both disharmony and evil.

It has been mistakenly reported that the Navajos have a terrible fear of death. Actually they have a tremendous respect for life, and an avoidance of the dead,[3] not a fear of death. Eighty-five-year-old singer, Bidaga, notes that he is getting old and it is time for him to die. He says that when he was young he wanted to live but with old age should come death. Death is described as the departing from the body of the breath (wind) of life. He notes that it is "just up to that wind when he will get out of the body, and then die. But this wind himself he knows just what year and what month and what time the person will die" (Ladd, 1957:417). In a study of Navajo philosophy, John Ladd (a philosopher himself) concluded that death per se was not considered evil or feared but that the desirability of a long life in effect meant the undesirability of dying before old age. *Death* as an experience is not feared. It is inastute contact with the dead that is avoided in order to prevent unnatural illness and premature death.

The term *są'ah*, therefore, expresses the Navajo concern for and emphasis upon life, and their attitude toward death of old age as a goal of life.

Naagháii

Naagháii is one of over three hundred thousand (356,200 by my calculation[4]) distinct conjugations of the verb 'to go'. This particular conjugation is the singular form of the third person of the continuative-imperfective mode, which refers to continually going about and returning. The prefix *naa-* of this verb is but one example of the great emphasis upon repetitions, continuations, and revolutions found in the Navajo language.

The Navajo verb distinguishes six modes and a number of aspects. Two of these modes and two of these aspects are concerned with the repetition, restoration, or continuous reoccurrence of an event or set of conditions, some of which imply the completion of a cycle or a revolution. There are also two verbal prefixes which denote various types of repetitions, restorations, or reoccurrences. One of these is the prefix *hi* which renders the idea of succession. An example of the use of this prefix with the verb 'to go' is *ahiikai* which translates 'we went in, or out of sight, one after another'. Reichard calls *hi* the "repetitive of action or motion" (1951:262).

The other verbal prefix of interest here is *náá* or *ná*. Reichard says that *náá* refers to the repetition of an act or condition, while *ná* refers to the restoration of a condition or an act, or to the completion of a revolution or a cycle (1951:220). Paul Platero, a Navajo linguist, believes that actually *náá* and *ná* are the same prefix, and that this prefix has either a long or short vowel depending on its position in a given verb or with what sounds it combines within a given verb (Platero, personal communication). This prefix can refer to either a repetition or a revolution. If used together (*nááná*), the semantic result is either a repetition of a repetition or a repetition of a revolution.

Restoration is a particularly important concept in understanding the nature and purpose of curing rites. Illness occurs when the normal harmony of one's world becomes disrupted, and curing rites are designed to restore harmony through which the health of the patient is also restored. These ceremonial restorations are indicated in Navajo language by the prefix *ná*.

Words, like thoughts, are considered to have creative power. In mythology things came into being or happened as people thought or talked about them. Repeating something four times will cause it to occur. A request made four times cannot be easily denied. At the end of each major portion of a ceremonial prayer, the phrase *hózhǫ náhásdlį́į'* is repeated four times. This phrase can be glossed here as 'harmony, beauty, and health have been restored'.

As mentioned before, the curing rites are designed to harmonize the patient with the world or his total environment. The world operates daily and yearly on the basis of a four-phased cycle. This is accomplished daily in the four-pointed path of the sun, and yearly in the four seasons of the annual cycle of the earth. Since the sun and the earth, days and years, operate according to a four-phased cycle, ritual drama designed to harmonize the patient's life with these important aspects of the universe must be repeated four times.

In the discussion above a particular view of action and being, repetition and reoccurrence, revolution and restoration was found to be implicit in Navajo verbal and ritual behavior, and these views and concepts are particularly relevant to an understanding of the symbolic meanings of the phrase *sǫ'ah naagháii bik'eh hózhǫ*.

Reichard observed that a basic Navajo belief is that "if something happened once, it may happen again" (1950a:13). I think we can go further than that and say that if something happens once, it is likely to happen again, and maybe even again and again. *Są'ah* refers to the completion of the life cycle through death of old age, and *naagháii* refers to the continual reoccurrence of the life cycle.

Bik'eh

Bik'eh is the easiest of the four terms to translate. It means 'according to it' or 'by its decree'. The *bi* (it) in this case refers to what preceded it, which is *są'ah naagháii*. What follows *bik'eh* is, then, the product of or exists in conjunction with *są'ah naagháii*. The by-product of *są'ah naagháii* is *hózhǫ*.

Hózhǫ

The term *hózhǫ* is most often translated as 'beauty', although all writers recognize that this term means much more than just 'beauty' or 'beautiful conditions'. Wyman translates *hózhǫ* as everything that the Navajo thinks of as being good—that is, good as opposed to evil, favorable to man as opposed to unfavorable. He feels it expresses such concepts as beauty, perfection, harmony, goodness, normality, success, well-being, blessedness, order and ideal (1970:7). Reichard defines this term as perfection so far as it is obtainable by man, and feels that it represents the end toward which not only man but also supernaturals and time and motion, institutions, and behavior strive (1950a:45).

In his work on Navajo philosophy, Clyde Kluckhohn comments on the meaning of this all-important term:

There are, however, some abstract words, extremely difficult to render adequately in English, which are of the greatest importance for the understanding of Navajo philosophy. Perhaps the most significant of these is conveyed by the Navajo root *hózhǫ*. This is probably the central idea in Navajo religious thinking. It occurs in the names of two important

ceremonials (Blessing Way and Beauty Way) and is frequently repeated in almost all prayers and songs. In various
contexts it is best translated as 'beautiful', 'harmonious',
'good', 'blessed', 'pleasant', and 'satisfying'. As a matter of
fact, the difficulty with translation primarily reflects the poverty of English in terms that simultaneously have moral and
esthetic meaning (1949:368–69).

The translations of Wyman, Reichard, and Kluckhohn provide
a good general notion of the meaning of hózhǫ́ but they are all
inadequate because they deal with only one of the two morpho-
logical components of the term. They take into account only the
meanings of the stem -zhǫ́, and ignore the semantic significance of
the prefix ho.[5] Ho is a verbal prefix used widely in Navajo language, but it has not been carefully defined by students of Navajo
language. The closest English gloss of ho might be 'environment',
considered in its total sense. When one is referring to environmental conditions as a whole, the term hoot'é is used. Ho contrasts
in meaning with the prefix ni which refers not to the total environment but to a particular item, event, or aspect of the environment. Thus when one says nizhóní he means 'it (something specific) is nice, pretty, good', whereas hózhóní means that everything
in the environment is nice, beautiful, and good. As a verbal prefix, ho refers to (1) the general as opposed to the specific; (2) the
whole as opposed to the part; (3) the abstract as opposed to the
concrete; (4) the indefinite as opposed to the definite; and (5) the
infinite as opposed to the finite (Witherspoon, 1974:53–54).

From the preceding discussion we can say that hózhǫ́ refers to
the positive or ideal environment. It is beauty, harmony, good,
happiness, and everything that is positive, and it refers to an
environment which is all-inclusive. Concepts of positive health or
well-being (shił hózhǫ́; shił yá'áhoot'ééh; hozhdiniilts'ííd) all use
the environment signifier ho. Positive health for the Navajo involves a proper relationship to everything in one's environment,
not just the correct functioning of one's physiology.

An opposite of hózhǫ́ is hóchxǫ' which could be glossed as 'the ugly, unhappy, and disharmonious environment'. It is not considered to be part of the natural cycle of the universe, and comes about only as a result of evil intentions and evil deeds. When it does occur, the normal condition of *hózhǫ* can be restored through the curing rites of the Navajo.

The goal of Navajo life in this world is to live to maturity in the condition described as *hózhǫ,* and to die of old age, the end result of which incorporates one into the universal beauty, harmony, and happiness described as *sǫ'ah naagháii bik'eh hózhǫ.*

Actually *Sǫ'ah Naagháii* and *Bik'eh Hózhǫ* are the central animating powers of the universe, and, as such, they produce a world described as *hózhǫ,* the ideal environment of beauty, harmony, and happiness. All living beings, which includes the earth, the sacred mountains, and so on, have inner and outer forms, and to achieve well-being the inner forms must harmonize and unify with *Sǫ'ah Naagháii* and the outer forms must harmonize and unify with *Bik'eh Hózhǫ.*

The desirable conditions of *sa'ah naagháii bik'eh hózhǫ* are disturbed and disrupted by improper, inadvertent, or inastute contact with things that are defined as dangerous (*báhádzid*), and by the malevolent deeds (witchcraft) of others. A variety of over sixty curing rites are designed to purify the patient made ill by contact with dangerous things or to neutralize and, in some cases, reverse the effects of witchcraft.

Curing rites, often referred to as "sings," reenact the creation of the world through myth, song, prayer, and drama, and place the patient in this recreated world, closely identifying him with the good and power of various deities. These deities are, in the words of Kluckhohn, "charged with positive spiritual electricity" (1949:370). Ritual identification with them neutralizes the contaminating effect of dangerous things or evil deeds and restores one to the good and harmony of *hózhǫ.*

In this connection I believe the metaphor using electricity is quite appropriate, and I would like to take it a little further. In doing so, I would describe *sǫ'ah naagháii bik'eh hózhǫ* as the generating plant or sources of animation and life for the inner forms of all living beings. The Holy People are supernaturals because of their closeness to these power sources and because of their knowledge of the ways (rituals) to connect to and harmonize with these central power sources. Reichard described this process as a kind of spiritual osmosis (1950a:112).

At this point some lines from Blessingway (Witherspoon, 1974:56–57; Wyman, 1970:134–36) would be helpful in illustrating the ritual process of restoration. In the following lines, repeated in both song and prayer, the patient is identified with the earth and, through the earth, with *Są'ah Naagháii Bik'eh Hózhǫ́:*

Earth's feet have become my feet
    by means of these I shall live on.
Earth's legs have become my legs
    by means of these I shall live on.
Earth's body has become my body
    by means of this I shall live on.
Earth's mind has become my mind
    by means of this I shall live on.
Earth's voice has become my voice
    by means of this I shall live on.
Earth's headplume has become my headplume
    by means of this I shall live on.
The cord-like extension from the top of its head
    is cord-like from the top of my head
    as by means of this I shall live on.
There are mountains encircling it and
    Hózhǫ́ extends up their slopes,
    by means of these it will be *hózhǫ́* as I shall live on.

Są'ah Naagháii Bik'eh Hózhǫ́ I shall be,
Before me it will be *hózhǫ́* as I live on,
Behind me it will be *hózhǫ́* as I live on,
Below me it will be *hózhǫ́* as I live on,
Above me it will be *hózhǫ́* as I live on.

Hózhǫ́ has been restored.
Hózhǫ́ has been restored.

Hózhǫ́ has been restored.
Hózhǫ́ has been restored.

The first stanza identifies the patient's outer form with the outer form of the earth, and this stanza is then followed by one which identifies the patient's inner form with the inner form of the earth, and through this channel, to the central generators, *Sǫ'ah Naagháii Bik'eh Hózhǫ́.*

> It is surprising, surprising . . . *yi ye*!
> It is the very inner form of Earth that continues
>   to move with me, that has risen with me,
>   that is standing with me, that indeed
>   remains stationary with me.
> Now it is the inner form of *Sǫ'ah Naagháii*
>   now *Bik'eh Hózhǫ́* that continues to move with me,
>   that has risen with me, that is standing with me,
>   that indeed remains stationary with me . . .
> (Witherspoon, 1974:56–57; Wyman, 1970:136).

Next the patient is identified with the inner forms of the mountains and other deities, and after each identification with these various beings, the patient is identified with *Sǫ'ah Naagháii Bik'eh Hózhǫ́*. *Sǫ'ah Naagháii Bik'eh Hózhǫ́* do not generate electricity, at least not in the Western sense of electricity, but do generate *hózhǫ́*. Connection to and harmony with generators of *hózhǫ́* will produce *hózhǫ́* in one's environment.

Now let us return from this detailed diversion into the general and specific meanings of *sǫ'ah naagháii bik'eh hózhǫ́* to the Navajo definition of *sǫ'ah naagháii* as thought and *bik'eh hózhǫ́* as speech. Thought is the power source of all creation, transformation, and regeneration. Songs sung by the *Diyin Dine'é* ("Supernaturals" or "Holy People") during the time they were organizing this world clearly express the power of directed thought:

> I plan for it, when I plan for it, it drops nicely into position
> just as I wish, *ni yo o*. Earth's support I first lean into posi-

tion. As I plan for long life-happiness it yields to my wish as it nicely drops into position, *ni yo o* (Wyman, 1970:115).

There is additional evidence from everyday life which indicates the power of thought. Navajos emphasize that if one thinks of good things and good fortune, good things will happen. If one thinks of bad things, bad fortune will be one's lot. In my first few years among the Navajo, I was constantly scolded for thinking about unhappy possibilities. As a product of another cultural world, I had learned to consider and plan for all possibilities and to "save something for a rainy day." Among the Navajo I was told that planning for that "rainy day" would bring about "rainy days," and that I had better forget about planning for "rainy days" unless I wanted it to "rain."

During my introduction to Navajo culture another matter that perplexed me was the seriousness with which Navajos regarded bad dreams. Bad dreams are regarded as bad thoughts likely to be realized unless treated and transformed through ritual action. To protect themselves from the dangerous potentialities of bad dreams and to prevent their reoccurrence (which would serve to reinforce them), Navajos make relatively large investments of time and money in ritual action.

During two different periods of severe drought on the reservation, people attributed the droughts to their bad, evil, improper, or disrespectful thoughts. People constantly reminded each other to think positively and to be respectful of the powers of the Holy People and their rites. Four times I observed the rain ceremony (*ntł'iz naha'nííł*) performed on days with clear skies, and each time it rained within twelve hours of the conclusion of the rite, which lasted only a few hours. Only once, however, was the rain significant enough to be of some help. The other times the rite, so it seemed, brought only a sprinkle of short duration. The Navajos involved in the performance of the rite shrugged their shoulders with a slight sense of humor and not a little dismay and commented, "How feeble-minded we have become!"

I have also observed cases where the curing rites failed to cure or where the blessing rites seemingly failed to bless. The explanations given in such cases fall into one or more of the following three categories: (1) the diagnosis was wrong; (2) a mistake was made in the performance of the ritual; or (3) the patient was not sincere, evidenced by his failure to follow all the prescriptions for and limitations on his behavior before, during, and after the rite.

Navajos believe strongly in the power of thought. The world was created by it; things are transformed according to it; life is regenerated from it. People are cured and blessed, vegetation is improved and increased, and health and happiness are restored by the power of thought.

Thought (sǫ'ah naagháii) is not without its inseparable companion, speech (bik'eh hózhǫ).According to the Navajo, speech is the outer form of thought, and thought is the inner form of speech. Before we can fully understand what it means in Navajo ideology to say that thought is the inner form of speech and speech is the outer form of thought, we must briefly consider the whole phenomenon of inner and outer forms.

Natural phenomena such as earth and sky, sun and moon, rain and water, lightning and thunder, and so on have inner forms. They are referred to as bii'astį 'an animate being lies within'. These 'in lying ones' are human-like in character and appearance, and retain their individual identity and agency. What First Man and First Woman and the others brought into being by their thoughts were the inner forms of all the natural phenomena that would be prominent in the structure and operation of this world (Wyman, 1970:109–12). After these inner forms were created in the sweathouse, they were told where their places would be and what their functions would be in the world, and then they were sent to take those positions and fill those functions.

People also have inner forms. These are referred to as nitch'i bii'sizíinii, usually translated as the 'in-standing wind soul'. The in-standing wind soul is thought to be in control of one's body, including one's thoughts and actions. The "goodness" or "badness" of a person is attributed to the nature of his wind soul. There are said to be seven general classes of wind souls, and a few other exceptional ones (in the sense of being either extremely good or extremely bad).

Like the inner forms of natural phenomena, these wind souls have an existence which is independent of the body which they occupy. They are dispatched into one's body at birth, and become its source of life and breath, thought and action. At death they leave the body and "return to dawn woman to report on the life of the person thus controlled" (Haile, 1943:87).

When the fetus acquires human form, a "small wind" is dispatched to it. This small wind is what causes the fetus to move, and its movements are evidence to the mother that the small wind has taken its place inside the growing fetus. The distinction between the "small wind" soul and the wind soul acquired at birth is important for understanding the nature of thought and speech. Haile states:

This soul [small wind] manifests its activity in "four speeches." These are found both in pre-natal movements of the child in the womb, and in post natal cries for nourishment, which approximate the call: šimá 'my mother'. T'was also told that this small wind "grows with a person," but does "not think far ahead." This "planning and calculating of things beneficial to the future of the individual" is done by the "wind placed into a person at birth." This tradition assigns a definite function to small winds, which seem to control the vegetative life of the human being, as "they grow with a person." This function is not replaced by the wind which, from birth on, does the planning "for the future" (1943:80).

The capacities to think "far ahead" and to speak a language are acquired from the wind soul dispatched at birth, and these capacities distinguish humans from other animals who have only calls and cries.

Whereas the little wind controls the digestive system of the body and, therefore, its growth and maturation, the in-standing wind soul controls one's thoughts and movements. Navajos believe that thought is located in the brain, but they contend that the in-stand-ing soul controls the functioning of the brain. Bodily movements, actions, or behavior are extensions or externalizations of thought. They are indeed external and observable evidence of the power of thought.

Speech is an externalization of thought. Being the outer form of thought, speech is an extension of thought. To the Navajo, speech represents marvelous evidence of the varied character and extensive capacity of thought. Moreover, speech is a reinforce-ment of the power of thought; it is an imposition on the external world. This reinforcement reaches its peak after four repetitions, and therefore a request made four times cannot be easily denied.

Although it was implied earlier (cf. p. 16) that this world was *thought* into existence, the consummation or realization of the thoughts of the Holy People did not occur until they were spoken in prayer or sung in song. Thought, the inner form, and speech, the outer form, represent the two basic components of ritual cre-ation or restoration. As we shall discuss later, thought is associated with form, and speech, as a kind of action, is associated with the transformation of substance (air); thus, ritual creation and resto-ration constitute a union of form and substance, or an imposition of form onto substance.

In the songs of creation referred to earlier, thought and speech were combined with another form or component of ritual action: knowledge. As thought precedes speech, knowledge precedes thought. Knowledge thus appears to be the inner form of thought. In this sense thought is the crystallization or conceptual-ization of knowledge.

As knowledge precedes thought, language precedes speech. In two of the best accounts of the origin myth (Goddard, 1933:9, 127; Haile, 1943), *saad ła'í* 'first language' is listed as one of the primordial elements of the universe. It is obvious to the Navajo that speech cannot occur unless a language already exists. As in all creations or transformations, form precedes substance, and lan-guage is associated with form and speech with substance.

It may seem perplexing to non-Navajos that thought, an inner form of speech, could be the outer form of knowledge and that speech, an outer form of thought, could be the outer form of language, but it is entirely consistent with the Navajo view of the world. Many inner forms also have inner forms of which they are outer forms. Included in this category are *Sǫ'ah Naagháii* 'thought' and *Bik'eh Hózhǫ́* 'speech'. Haile's informant states that the in-standing wind soul (inner form) of *Sǫ'ah Naagháii* is the 'inaudible wind', and the in-standing wind soul (inner form) of *Bik'eh Hózhǫ́* is 'smooth wind' (1973:74).

The names of the wind souls interestingly parallel or character-ize their nature and function. Haile's translation of *niłch'i doo diits'a'ígíí* as 'inaudible wind' is misleading. First, *niłch'i* is 'air' and not necessarily 'wind'. Second, *doo diits'a'ígíí* means 'that which makes no noise' or 'the silent one' instead of 'inaudible' which suggests it makes a noise but its noise cannot be heard. Knowl-edge, the inner form of thought, obviously makes no noise. It seems appropriate, therefore, that the inner form of *sǫ'ah naagháii* is a soul that makes no noise. It is also interesting to note that an 'inaudible wind' soul is the inner form of white wind, which is the inner form of dawn, the beginning point of the day, and east, the correct starting point of the four cardinal directions. All four-phased prayers to the cardinal points begin with dawn or east, whose color is white. In the four phases of creation or trans-formation, the beginning phase is knowledge.

The in-standing soul of *Bik'eh Hózhǫ́* is 'smooth wind', according to Haile's translation. In Navajo conception 'smoothness' implies form or pattern. Again Haile's translation is inadequate. *Niłch'i diilkǫǫh* means 'the air or wind that has been smoothed', not 'smooth wind'. The "smoothing" process relates to the Navajo conception of what happens to air when it becomes articulated sound. It appears, then, that the name 'smoothed wind' for the inner form of *Bik'eh Hózhǫ́* (speech) is not arbitrary but is illustra-tive of the patterning role that language plays in speech.

From the propositions that knowledge is the inner form of thought, language is the inner form of speech, and thought is the inner form of speech, it may be presumed that knowledge is also the inner form of language. The structural arrangement of these components is diagrammed in figure 1. This structural arrangement illustrates how all ritual creation or restoration begins with knowledge and culminates in speech. For the Navajo, then, knowledge is power, and the greatest power to transform or restore various conditions comes from the knowledge of various rituals acquired from the Holy People. As such, ritual knowledge is highly treasured and not easily obtained.

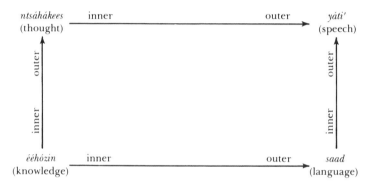

Fig. 1. Structural Relationships among Knowledge, Language, Thought, and Speech (*Adapted from Witherspoon, 1975b:75*)

Ritual knowledge can be purchased but it cannot be produced; it can be learned but it cannot be discovered; it can be communicated but it cannot be destroyed. Ritual knowledge is fixed and complete; it cannot be expanded. All there is to know about this world is already known because the world was organized according to this knowledge. Earth surface people (Navajos or human beings) can expand their awareness or command of knowledge, but they cannot expand knowledge itself.

Creation is the external manifestation of knowledge. When asked what they were planning in the sweathouse, the Holy People said, "we are planning to extend knowledge endlessly" (Goddard, 1933:26, my translation). In Navajo mythology there are four underworlds (sometimes extended to twelve when phases within the principal underworlds are enumerated) that preceded this, the fifth world. The first of these underworlds is called *saad* ła'í 'first language', the second is called *saad naakií* 'second language', and so on (Haile, 1949:3). At first glance this description of the underworlds may sound strange but if we recognize that language is the means by which form is projected onto substance, we can see that these underworlds are really being described as "first form," "second form," and so on.

Navajos do not postulate the possibility that language may distort reality or our perception of reality. Such a proposition goes directly contrary to the Navajo scheme of things. This world was transformed from knowledge, organized in thought, patterned in language, and realized in speech (symbolic action). The symbol was not created as a means of representing reality; on the contrary, reality was created or transformed as a manifestation of symbolic form. *In the Navajo view of the world, language is not a mirror of reality; reality is a mirror of language.*

The language of Navajo ritual is performative (Austin, 1962), not descriptive. Ritual language does not describe how things are; it determines how they will be. Ritual language is not impotent; it is powerful. It commands, compels, organizes, transforms, and restores. It disperses evil, reverses disorder, neutralizes pain, overcomes fear, eliminates illness, relieves anxiety, and restores order, health, and well-being.

The language of Navajo ritual has been an enigma to most scholars because the philosophy of language they have used to interpret Navajo ritual behavior has gone directly contrary to the Navajo philosophy of language. I will now try to outline briefly the nature, function, and effectiveness of ritual language. This will be done in light of the Navajo philosophy of language.

The primary purpose of Navajo ritual is to maintain or restore *hózhǫ́*. As discussed earlier, *hózhǫ́* is everything that is good, harmonious, orderly, happy, and beautiful. The opposite of *hózhǫ́* is *hóchxǫ'* which, of course, is the evil, the disorderly, and the ugly. Navajo rituals can be divided into three general kinds, depending on how they maintain, insure, or restore *hózhǫ́*. The first of these, the Blessingway rites (*Hózhǫ́ǫ́jí*), maintain and reinforce *hózhǫ́* by attracting and incorporating the goodness and power of benevolent Holy People. A second general type of ritual, the Holyway rites (*Diyink'ehgo*), deals with Holy People who are potentially malevolent. These rites emphasize transformation; that is, transforming powers that are potentially malevolent and dangerous into benevolent powers. This is done by ritual control and compulsion, creating in the patient an immunity to the potential evil of the Holy Person thus controlled. A third general class of ritual, the Evilway rites (*Hóchxǫ'íjí*), emphasizes the exorcism of the evil powers of malevolent Holy People, thus eliminating *hóchxǫ'* and restoring *hózhǫ́*.

At the core of Navajo ritual is the relationship between the *Diyin Dine'é* 'Holy People' and the *nihokáá dine'é* 'earth surface people'. *Diyin* may be translated as 'immune' for the Holy People are immune to danger, destruction, and death as a reflection of their inherent knowledge. Earth surface people may incorporate this power and immunity by knowing how to control and compel the Holy People who possess it. The symbolic action of ritual is the process by which the Holy People are controlled and compelled.

In most cases the Holy People of the fifth world are the inner forms of various natural phenomena and forces, including animals, and are the controlling and animating powers of nature. Navajo ritual is not designed to control the elements directly; it is designed to control the Holy People who are the inner forms and controlling agents of those elements.

The goal of the earth surface people is to die of old age after a long life of beauty, harmony, and happiness. This must be accomplished, however, in a world of benevolent and malevolent forces. To reach old age one must identify with and incorporate the good of benevolent powers and transform or exorcise the evil of malevolent powers.

The inner forms of various natural phenomena are humanoid. They can hear the speech of ritual and can see the movements and prestations involved in the symbolic action of ritual. These inner forms (in-lying ones) of natural phenomena also have inner forms (in-standing wind souls). Just as with the earth surface people, it is the nature or class of the in-standing wind soul that determines whether the particular Holy Person is benevolent, malevolent, or a combination of these.

This world is an arena in which the inner forms of the Holy People and the inner forms of the earth surface people interact. This is manifested in the movements and interactions of their outer forms. Since the movements of outer forms are representations of the thoughts and intents of inner forms, these actions or interactions are symbolic in nature. The world is, therefore, a stage of symbolic action. One of the most important aspects of symbolic action is found in language, and it is that aspect of symbolic action toward which our attention is focused in this chapter.

Songs of Blessingway illustrate the pattern of identifying with and incorporating the good of benevolent Holy People. Earth Woman is a Holy Person who is incapable of doing harm to anyone. She is only capable of blessing, aiding, and sustaining; and, as such, is the very essence of benevolence. The following excerpts from Blessingway songs illustrate how the patient identifies with and incorporates the benevolent power of Earth Woman:

> As I stand along the surface of the Earth
> she says child to me, she says grandchild to me. . . .
>
> Now at Earth's soles, now dark cloud,
> now male rain, now dark water,
> rainbow, now pollen usually lies across.
>
> Now at my soles, now dark cloud,
> now male rain, now dark water,
> rainbow, now pollen usually lies across. . . .
> (Wyman, 1970:123, 128)

(This is followed by similar verses which make an identification with the tips of Earth's toes, the tips of her knees, the palms of her hands, her fingertips, the tip of her body, the tips of her shoulders, her cheeks, eyes, lips, and finally the top of her head.)

The verses above constitute an identification of outer forms. This is followed by an identification of inner forms:

> It is the very inner form of Earth that continues to move with me, that has risen with me, that is standing with me, that indeed remains stationary with me (Wyman, 1970:136).

The prayers of the holy way chants are designed to transform evil and gain immunity from evil. To illustrate this process the following excerpts from the Male Shootingway are provided:

At Rumbling Mountain,
Holy Man who with the eagle tail-feathered arrow glides out,
   This day I have come to be trustful
   This day I look to you. . . .
With your strong feet rise up to protect me,
With your sturdy legs rise up to protect me,
With your strong body rise up to protect me,
With your healthy mind rise up to protect me,
With your powerful sound rise up to protect me,
Carrying the dark bow and the eagle tail-feathered arrow
with which you transformed evil,
   By these means you will protect me,
. . . .
No weapon of evil sorcery can harm me as I go about.
   This day I shall recover.
   Safely may I go about.
   Your child I have become,
   Your grandchild I have become,
   I have recovered my energy, I say.
. . . .
Just as you are the one who is holy because of these things,
   So may I be holy because of them.
. . . .
This day the weapon of sorcery
   Has returned to normal.
. . . .
Just as you are the one who transforms evil,
   So may I transform evil.

Just as you are the one dreaded by evil because of these things,
So may I be dreaded by evil because of these things.
. . . .
We all survive.
My mind in safety repeatedly survives.
. . . .
[*Sǫ'ah naagháíí bik'eh hózhǫ́*] I have become again.
. . . .
It has become beautiful again. . . . (Reichard, 1944:58–65)

The Evilway rites are designed to exorcise evil from the patient's body, mind, and presence. To illustrate how ritual language is used in this process, the following excerpts from an Evilway rite, Enemyway, are provided:

From where threatens the weapon of the white man's ghost,
its sorcery, its indispensable power, its parts naturally affected by evil, all of which bother me inside my body, which
make me feverish, move deceitfully through me,
    From there may they be warned off (by winking), far away
    may they go,
    Along with its power of motion evil sorcery is moving far
    from me,
    Along with its power of motion its threatening sound is
    moving far from me,
    Far away with its evil power it has gone.
    It has gone back to its own dwelling place,
    It has become unknown water.   (Reichard, 1944:31)
    . . . .

In the translations above Reichard frequently includes "may"
which gives a misleading sense of asking for permission. There is
no "may" or requesting of permission in the Navajo versions.
Phrases such as "so may I be dreaded by evil" should read "so I
will be dreaded by evil."

There is another important source of *hóchxǫ'* that must be
brought under control and reversed or neutralized. It is found in

witchcraft, and has been part of the world from the beginning, having been part of the knowledge of First Man and First Woman. Witchcraft is associated with incest, and First Man and First Woman are both brother and sister and husband and wife to each other. First Man is said to be the originator of "invisible witchcraft," and First Woman is the originator of "noisy medicine" and "gray witchcraft" (Haile, 1943:75).

The children of First Man and First Woman are called *Áńt'įįhjí Są'ah Naagháii* and *Áńt'įįhjí Bik'eh Hózhǫ*. *Áńt'įįhjí* is 'witchcraft', and these children, born of incest, are personifications of witchery *są'ah naagháii* 'thought' and witchery *bik'eh hózhǫ* 'speech'. Whereas *Są'ah Naagháii* plus *Bik'eh Hózhǫ* produce, maintain, and restore *hózhǫ*, witchery *Są'ah Naagháii* plus witchery *Bik'eh Hózhǫ* produce *hóchxǫ'*. One of the most common ways of producing *hóchxǫ'* is by reversing the order and sequence of the rites which produce *hózhǫ*. Reichard notes that "the power of the word is as strong for evil as for good, an inverse wish being a curse" (1950a:275). Haile adds:

The colored winds, too, which are assigned in proper sequence to the phenomena of the cardinal points, to wit: white wind soul to dawn, blue wind soul to horizontal blue, yellow wind soul to evening twilight, dark wind soul to darkness, are considered benevolent, if mentioned in this sequence in religious functions. But when a ceremonial, in its songs and prayers, disturbs this sequence, giving preference to darkness, malevolence and witchery may be suspected (1943:75).

Whereas ritual language can be used to create order, it can also be used to create disorder. Ritual language was the means of transforming chaos into cosmos, but it can also be used to reduce cosmos to chaos. In the battle between the forces of disorder and evil and those of order and good, the "good" side has the advantage. This is based on the idea that through ritual knowledge and circumspect behavior one can acquire an immunity from evil, but there is no immunity from the ritual control and compulsion of good. There are no evil forces or deities that cannot be transformed or exorcised.

Evil and malevolence also have an advantage. They act secretly and deceptively. Before one can transform, exorcise, or reverse evil, one must know its nature and source. This is the function of the diviner or diagnostician. Often, however, serious misfortune or death is caused before the nature and source of the evil is discovered. If the source of the problem is witchcraft and the witch is discovered, the witch will die because his evil power can be reversed and returned. There is only one escape from this pronounced doom. He can acknowledge his misdeeds and be treated by a holy way rite by which he can gain an immunity from the evil forces that he himself has set in motion.

At this point I would like to summarize and clarify Navajo theories of knowledge, language, thought, and speech, and relate these theories to some of those found in linguistics. Navajos have distinct terms for each of these four aspects of the world, and they make rather sharp distinctions between and among them. Nevertheless, they also see important relationships among them, and see in them four paired sets.

Wilhelm von Humboldt, a linguist and philosopher of language of the nineteenth century, offered a view of thought and speech that interestingly parallels the Navajo view. He clearly saw thought as the director of speech, and speech as the external manifestation of thought:

Intellectual activity—completely intellectual, completely innate, and to a certain extent passing without a trace—becomes externalized in speech and perceptible to the senses. It and the language [which he equates with speech], therefore, are a unit and are indivisible from one another (1971:34).

Elsewhere he added that "language is, as it were, the external manifestation of the minds of peoples" (1971:24).

Like the Navajos, Humboldt saw air as an appropriate medium through which thought is externalized in speech:

> Inasmuch as thought in its most typically human relationships is a longing to escape from darkness into light, from limitation into infinity, sound streams from the depths of the breast to the external ambient. There it finds in the air, this most subtle and motile of all elements whose apparent incorporeality significantly corresponds to the intellect, a marvelously appropriate intermediary substance. . . . For, as living sound, it proceeds, as does respiration itself, from the breast . . . breathing life from which it streams forth into the mind which receives it. . . . Thus it connects man with the universe (1971:34–35).

In Navajo conception thought is not an aspect of the small wind soul which is received prenatally and controls the digestive system, but is rather a dimension of the in-standing wind soul which is received at birth and controls respiration and is the source and medium of speech (Haile, 1943:80). Reichard lists numerous terms which illustrate a close association of life, breath, and speech with air (1944:51–52). Although Humboldt did not project the existence of an "in-standing wind soul" as the source of speech, he did postulate something similar to it, although he did not elaborate on its nature or composition. He stated that human speech is "the organ of the internal being, this self that progressively achieves internal cognition and enunciation" (1971:xix).

In line with the Navajo philosophy of language, Humboldt also saw the ultimate effect of thought and speech as making an impact on the form and events of the world:

> The truly creative principle operating in the recondite and secret course of mankind's development is the power of the intellect which sallies forth from its inner depth and plentitude to intervene in the events of the world (1971:7).

Elsewhere he added:

> The intellect produces, but stands in contrast to, the created item. . . . Thus from the cosmos reflected in man originates . . . the language which associates him with his environment and which, through his effort, reacts fruitfully upon the latter (1971:163).

Humboldt's view and the Navajo view part company with regard to the distinction between language and speech. Humboldt made little distinction between language and speech. This is probably due to his view that the form and content of both language and speech are products of the intellect. To him the intellect is both the originator of language and the director of speech.

Until now we have not distinguished *saad* as 'word' or 'words' from *saad* as 'language'. Because there is no such overt distinction in the Navajo language, most scholars have assumed that Navajos make no such distinction. Reichard argues strongly that such conclusions are not necessarily warranted. She states:

> . . . Navajo language is every bit as subtle as English, if not more so. . . . One apparent feature of the language is what one might call a "linguistic synecdoche," that is, the designation of a whole and a part, or selected parts, by the same term. For instance the same word is used to name a medicine bundle with all its contents, the skin (quiver) in which the contents are wrapped, the contents as a whole or each part of the contents (1944:38).

As in Reichard's example of the medicine bundle, *saad* may refer to both 'language' as a system, and to 'words' as parts of that system. Navajos refer to the 'Navajo language' as *Diné bizaad,* to Spanish as *Naakaii* (Mexican) *bizaad* (his language), and to English as the *saad* of the white man. This clearly indicates that Navajos see these languages as systems of words. There are a multitude of ways to identify individual words or groups of words. One can speak a sentence and most any Navajo can count the number of *saad* in the sentence.

One can say *Dinék'ehjí yáshti'* which translates 'according to the Navajo pattern, I speak'. I once heard a Navajo comment on the incorrect syntax used by a non-Navajo trying to speak Navajo. He said, *Dinék'ehjígo dóó ákot'áo saad ałkéé sinil da,* which translates 'according to the form of Navajo (speaking), words are not ordered in that way'. From the foregoing evidence I think it is clear that Navajos use *saad* to refer both to language as a system and as a whole, and to words as elements of the system and parts of the whole. It is also clear that they see form and pattern as inherent qualities of language.

Just as the inner parts of a medicine bundle are called *jish* (the same term as that used for the medicine bundle itself), the inner parts or elements of language are called *saad.* According to Navajo mythology, *saad* ("words, symbols, or names") are considered to be one of the primordial elements of the universe, antedating the existence of First Man and First Woman (Goddard, 1933:9, 127). Thus *saad* as words or symbols precede *saad* as patterned whole or grammar and constitute the inner form of the latter.

Ééhózin 'knowledge' is the awareness of thing or being and its symbolic representation. To a great extent, the beginning of man's knowledge is found in learning the natures and names of things. Unlike Adam, First Man did not go about naming things (creating symbols); he went about learning the names of things (interpreting reality through already established symbols).

Although First Man and First Woman were not the originators or inventors of symbol, they were the originators of form. The capacity to organize, arrange, and pattern symbols is found in the intellect. Symbols are the building blocks of mental images, and just as man cannot build a house without materials, so man cannot construct mental images of the universe without symbolic elements.

This is not to say that in the Navajo view man cannot or does not create symbols. After symbols have been organized in thought, and this organization or form has been imposed on substance, a new symbol is needed to symbolize the new world, and it is man who finds or creates a symbol to represent his own creations. This new or additional symbol becomes part of his symbolic resources for future thought and creation. The present world is the fifth world; it is organized out of symbols that originated and developed in the four underworlds. Each of these successive worlds, except the first underworld, was organized out of the symbols of previous worlds. The first underworld had substance but it possessed no inherent form. Because the capacity to originate and impose form is inherent in the intellect, First Man and First Woman imposed form onto the substance of the first world. Things do not think; symbols do not think—man thinks.

Having acquired the capacity to impose form and order onto the world, First Man and First Woman also acquired the capacity to return order to disorder, cosmos to chaos. Whereas *sǫ'ah naagháii* 'thought' and *bik'eh hózhǫ́* 'speech' produce *hózhǫ́*, *áńt'į́įhjí* (witchery) *sǫ'ah naagháii* and *bik'eh hózhǫ́* produce *hóchxǫ'*. *Hózhǫ́* may be conceived of as the imposition of form, order, harmony, beauty, and, therefore, good upon the world. When *hóchxǫ'* occurs in one's world, it is as though things have returned to original chaos. The ritual takes the patient back to the beginning of things, or apparently it assumes he is already there because it is there that the ritual starts, and recreates the world according to *hózhǫ́*. Ritual reinforms the environment with harmony, order, and beauty, and that is why all rituals conclude with the phrase "*hózhǫ́* has been restored."

The original creation of *hózhǫ́* was a development of thought and intellect on the part of the Holy People. For the earth surface people, restoration of *hózhǫ́* is a dimension or capacity of ritual knowledge. The Navajo term *ééhózin* ("knowledge") really means 'awareness', 'acquaintance', or 'familiarity'. Awareness of thing or being is the core of ritual knowledge, and might well be considered its inner form. When the inner forms of knowledge and language are added to the structure found in figure 1, the result is the structure illustrated in figure 2. This figure represents my logical extension of the Navajo concepts discussed in this chapter.

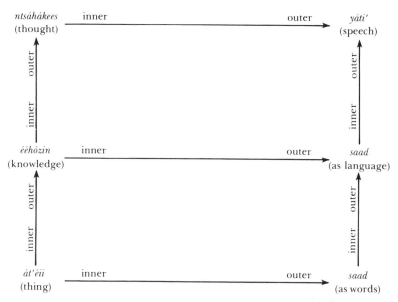

Fig. 2. Structural Relationships among Thing, Word, Knowledge, Language,
Thought, and Speech (*Adapted from Witherspoon, 1975b:85*)

The arrows in figure 2 are used only to represent the inner/
outer structural relationships between and among all the categories. Actually the two entities at each level (thing and word,
knowledge and language, thought and speech) form a pair, and
the lower pairs are the inner forms of the next higher pair. Because each of these pairs has an inner and an outer form and
because in ritual performances inner forms precede outer forms,
the correct sequential process of the structure appears to proceed
from the inner form of the lower pair to its outer form, then to
the inner form of the next pair and then to its outer form, and so
on. This is illustrated in figure 3. This model is based on structural relationships which are implicit in Navajo thought.

Many scholars see language as the creation of the intellect, but
the Navajos see that as putting the cart before the horse. To the
Navajo, man can think only with symbols, so some symbols must
have existed before thought. The first few sentences of the first

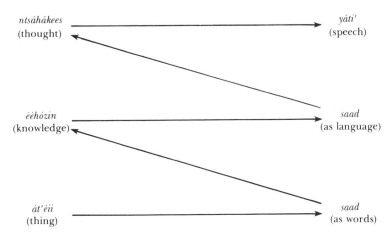

Fig. 3. Sequential Patterns among Thing, Word, Knowledge, Language, Thought, and Speech (*Adapted from Witherspoon, 1975b:86*)

paragraph of the emergence myth read: "The one that is called 'water everywhere'. The one that is called 'black earth'. The one that is called 'first language' " (my translation of the Navajo text recorded in Goddard, 1933:8). These phrases are significant in that they indicate that in the beginning were the word and the thing, the symbol, and the object. The Holy People first became *aware* of things through their symbols, and then later went into the sweathouse and organized these symbols through thought processes. Next the organized symbols were spoken in prayer and sung in song. Through these songs and prayers the inner forms of things to be were organized and controlled; that is, told where to go, how to position themselves, and what functions to fulfill.

Knowledge is the awareness of symbol, thought is the organization of symbol, speech is the externalization of symbol, and compulsion is the realization of symbol. Symbol is word, and word is the means by which substance is organized and transformed. Both substance and symbol are primordial, for in the beginning were the word and the element, the symbol and the symbolized.

CHAPTER 2

Controlling the World
through Language

In chapter 1 we discovered that for the Navajo the world was actually created or organized by means of language. The form of the world was first conceived in thought, and then this form was projected onto primordial unordered substance through the compulsive power of speech and song. Rappaport has referred to this process as the informing of substance and the substantiation of form (1974:42–46). Despite their appeal on aesthetic grounds, these metaphysical propositions seem very strange to people grounded in occidental philosophy, and thus any discussion of them is quickly classed as, at best, mystical or, at worst, magical. We refer to the powers Navajos attribute to thoughts and words as magical because we cannot understand them and cannot accept them on empirical or rational grounds. To Navajos, however, the powers of thought and speech are not particularly mysterious or magical because they simply follow logically from more fundamental premises on which the Navajo world was built and according to which it operates.

In this book I am more interested in what the Navajo think than in how they think. I believe the differences found in what we think and what they think are attributable not to any differences in intelligence or mental structures, or to some projected state of preliterate mentality, and certainly not to any supposed forms of "primitive" consciousness, but are attributable to different premises about the nature and operation of reality. These premises on which Navajo thinking is based are not assumed to be the same for all non-Western peoples, nor do I assume that many of these premises are not to be found in the Western world; what I do say is that they are given special and possibly unique articulation by the Navajo. And, of course, it is the world as articulated by the Navajo that is of specific interest to us here.

A Navajo premise that is significant and relevant to the powers of thought and speech is that all matter and all being have a dualistic nature: static and active. The assumption that underlies this dualistic aspect of all being and existence is that the world is in motion, that things are constantly undergoing processes of transformation, deformation, and restoration, and that the essence of life and being is movement. The static dimension is defined in terms of the active dimension, and is defined as the temporary withdrawal of motion; that is, something that is temporarily at rest in between its various movements. These propositions are very firmly and clearly embedded in the structure and content of Navajo language, ritual, myth, and art.

Both Reichard (1949) and Hoijer (1964) have written excellent and detailed articles that discuss the semantic dimensions of Navajo verb stems. They both conclude, even though their classes and labels are somewhat different, that there is a basic distinction between active and static (or neuter) verbs, and that overwhelming emphasis is given to the active verb, with the static side being defined by and in relation to the active.

Reichard begins her analysis by noting a marked division in Navajo verbs: verbs of condition or state (which she calls "static") and verbs of motion or action. It should be pointed out here that this distinction is particularly significant because of the astonishing degree to which the Navajo language is dominated by verbs. There seem to be few, if any, nouns that are not either passive forms of verbs or derived from verbal forms. Particles, prefixes, and postpositions are used primarily as verbal modifiers. The dominance of verbs in Navajo also corresponds to the Navajo emphasis on a world in motion. As mentioned earlier, I once conservatively estimated that Navajo contained some 356,200 distinct conjugations of the verb "to go." These conjugations all apply to the ways in which humans normally "go." If we added all the verbs relating "to move," as well as "to go" such as in walking or running, the number of conjugations would be well into the millions. In this regard it is particularly relevant and significant that the principal verb in the Navajo language is the verb "to go" and not the verb "to be," which is the principal verb in so many other languages but is of relatively minor importance in Navajo. This seems to indicate a cosmos composed of processes and events, as opposed to a cosmos composed of facts and things.

Static verbs describe the state, position, or condition of something that is temporarily at rest. The assumption is that nothing is totally inactive; in fact, everything exhibits both active and static characteristics. In the next chapter we will discuss how various entities in the world are classified according to their degree of inherent activity. Reichard notes that the understanding of active verbs and their variations of subject, object, agent, and aspect will be greatly increased if the verb is thought of as essentially emphasizing a kind of motion. She maintains that "once this idea is grasped and the general meaning of the stem is ascertained, the forms usually seem reasonable, whereas if one personalizes the forms and moves out from the subject instead of the abstraction of impersonal motion, the forms may make little sense and seem impossible to interpret" (1949:56).

Reichard shows that the idea of unrestricted motion progressing through space with only a peripheral reference to time is a significant aspect of Navajo verbs. This is especially found in the progressive-continuative system of verb stems, but it also appears in the inceptive forms. The inceptive relates the beginning, the end, and the space covered by an action or motion. She argues that the progressive-continuative system is so closely related to the inceptive that the feeling of the one is carried over to the other, resulting in small but significant gradations of kind and type of movement. For example, the progressive completive (*yi* perfective) 'it has been moving' compares to the inceptive completive (*ni* perfective) 'motion started for a goal is completed, has arrived, is finished' (1949:61).

Reichard divides all Navajo verb stems into the following semantic categories:

a. general stems, b. stems descriptive of a motion, an object in motion or both, c. stems descriptive of a motion, of an object in motion or both, but the motion being conceived of as taking place swiftly, suddenly, vigorously or forcefully, d. stems indicating body action or motion, e. stems indicating processes or construction, f. stems indicating senses or perceptions, g. stems indicating mental attitudes, emotions, behavior (1949:61).

The first of these categories is the most difficult to describe because it includes such stems as (-*ááł*) 'round object moves' which connotes many actions and movements not clearly associated with its apparent base referent. These include to owe, drink to excess, be ill, dip food, decide, act desperately, play shinny, emulate, sing, transfer knowledge, perform ritual, plan, discuss. Moreover, stems such as -*tįįł* 'rigid object moves' may refer to rituals and -*ááł* may refer to the formulation of plans.

Category (b) listed above is the most numerous category of verbs. Reichard notes that the object referred to by static verbs "is assumed to have power to move, or to be moved by a subject, agent or cause; this power is expressed by the verb of motion" (1949:62). She adds that whether the potential for motion is inherent or initiated by an agent is important in understanding the meanings of various stems in this category. She then provides a long list of object classes that seem to have an inherent capacity for motion, and thus do not require a moving agent. An example here would be *yitįįł* 'a long narrow, rigid object moves progressively' (1949:62).

Category (c) listed above is similar to category (b), with the addition of an adverbial modifier, referring to forceful, precipitous, or compulsive action.

Some stems of swift motion are: 'weight (in sense of mass) moves forcefully' (-*das*); 'object moves swiftly of its own weight' (as tree, apple falling) (-*tsił*); 'long, narrow, flexible object moves swiftly' (-*dił*); 'elastic object is moved forcefully' (as drumskin) (-dǫ́·ł); 'small object moves swiftly, suddenly because of applied force' (as bullet, foot kicking) (-tał); 'round object moves with force' (-tł'it); 'pecking, flipping motion' (-tąš) (1949:64).

The few examples listed here should illustrate how so many events are described in terms of the movements of various classes of objects.

Category (d) deals with body motion, and covers a wide variety of bodily movements, some of which are somewhat surprising. For example, Reichard notes that "one reason that Navajo has always seemed so hard to learn is that apparently simple examples in English are least typical in Navajo. One gets into difficulties with the verb 'see,' for which Navajo has several stems, none exactly equivalent; they too illustrate the exaggeration of motion" (1949:67). For example, -'įįł means 'sight moves, get sight in motion, bring into vision against, focus against'. The stem -tsééł also refers to seeing but it is cessative, 'pause in sighting'. Another stem -ghał refers to the rolling of one's eyes, and -gesh refers to staring, gazing abstractedly.

In category (e) we have stems which refer to processes and transformations. These include verbs that refer to construction, transformation, order, change, growth, maturation, birth, decay, disintegration, deformation, and so on. Stems in category (f) indicate sense and perception. In discussing this category Reichard makes the comment:

> Stems referring to sense and perception are particularly interesting in view of the old theory, still held by some, that primitive minds are apperceptive rather than conceptive. Tho most other stem categories already discussed are large, this class is very small. Some ideas that we should classify here, such as seeing, belong more properly to the category of motion. A stem (-dla·ł) that indicates penetration of the atmosphere seems to denote a process rather than a perception, since it means 'bright light, harsh sound rips (the air)'.

It is perhaps true that even the stems listed in this category are primarily verbs of motion insofar as the idea is compatible with the expression of sensibility (1949:71).

Hoijer (1964:143) divides Navajo verbs into two major categories: neuter and active. He notes that while the neuter verbs are conjugated in only one paradigm, active verbs require seven paradigms (imperfective, perfective, progressive, future, iterative, customary, optative). Neuter verbs imply an absence or withdrawal of motion, while active verbs report events, movements, and actions (1964:144). The active paradigms include the imperfective, *nìndàah* 'he moves to a sitting position'; the perfective, *nìńdá* 'he has moved to a sitting position'; the future, *nìndàah dòò* 'he will be moving to a sitting position'; the progressive, *nòòdààł* 'he goes along moving to a sitting position' (a better example here would be *yòò'àáł* 'he moves along holding in suspension a round, solid object'); the iterative, *nìnádààh* 'he moves to a sitting position repeatedly'; the inceptive progressive, *nìdòòdààł* 'he will start moving to a sitting position'.

Hoijer concludes from this discussion that Navajo verb categories "center very largely about the reporting of events, or better, 'eventings.' These eventings are divided into neuters, eventings solidified, as it were, into states by the withdrawal of motion, and actives, eventings in motion" (1964:145). He further notes that these movements are conceived of as the movements of corporeal bodies, or as entities metaphorically linked with corporeal bodies. The movement itself is reported in painstaking detail. In addition, Hoijer illustrates how "prefixes and prefix combinations, like the themes we have just cited, also refer in large part to movement" (1964:145).

Hoijer finds that a third pattern in Navajo speech further emphasizes movement. He refers to the technique of reporting substantive concepts in terms of some characteristic action or movement of an object or set of objects. Hoijer summarizes his presentation as follows:

. . . in three broad speech patterns, illustrated by the conjugation of active verbs, the reporting of actions and events, and the framing of substantive concepts, Navajo emphasizes movement and specifies the nature, direction, and status of such movement in considerable detail. Even the neuter category is relatable to the dominant conception of a universe in motion; for, just as someone is reported to have described architecture as frozen music, so the Navajo define position as a resultant of the withdrawal of motion (1964:146).

Movement and life seem to be inseparably related, if not equivalent. Movement is the basis of life, and life is exemplified by movement. Young and Morgan translate the meaning of the stem *naał* as "a stem which has to do with movement, life and duration" (1943:145). Combined with various prefixes, this stem expresses the meanings 'to be alive', 'to resuscitate, to come back to life', 'to endure, to last', 'to be fast (at thinking or in actions)', or 'to move some part of the body'. Interestingly enough this stem is also used to refer to the generation of electricity, which literally translated means 'to give it life'.

There is also a close relationship between sound and movement, and between sound and life. The verb stem *-ts'iił* means 'to move sound'. Young and Morgan say the literal translation of *naanáhosoolts'įįł* is 'sound is moving about' (1951:199). An infant is not considered to be alive until it has uttered a sound, and there is no customary burial or period of mourning for an infant who dies without uttering a sound. As we shall see later, a child does not acquire human status until he or she masters the art of speaking a language. It is clear from this that the Navajo consider speech to be a highly refined form of movement, and that speech is not only characteristic of, but necessary to, human life.

Having established that the Navajo world is a cosmos of motion and process, and that movement is fundamental to life and a characteristic of sound, the question that now arises is this: What is the source or power of movement? The answer to this question is air, for air is the only substance or entity in the Navajo world that has the inherent capacity to move and to bear knowledge. Air is the ultimate source of all knowledge and animation. Because knowledge cannot be transformed into action without going through thought, air is also the source of all thought.

It will be recalled from the last chapter that it is the "small wind (or air) soul" that enters the embryo and causes the fetus to grow. This air soul continues to control the vegetative system of the body. The "in-standing wind soul" is acquired at birth and controls one's thoughts, speech, and actions. When a person's breath leaves him, he dies; that is, he loses the capacity to move. Without air in the body the digestive and respiratory systems cannot function, the mind cannot think, and the body cannot produce sound or movement. The body has no inherent capacity for thought, speech, or movement; it acquires these capacities from air. A baby who never receives an "in-standing wind soul" is born still and silent—without life. In considering his own forthcoming death, eighty-five-year-old singer, Bidaga, noted that it is "just up to that wind when he will get out of the body, and then die. But this wind himself he knows just what year and what month and what time the person will die" (Ladd, 1957:417). This passage also suggests the inherent knowledge that air possesses.

Reichard notes that "one of Wind's functions is to give life (motion). Little Winds, crossing inside the newly made bodies, enabled the Navajo to stand up, and body hair to grow out of their pores" (1950a:497). Air also has lifting or supporting power (1950a:498).

Air is not only the source of human life and animation; it is also the source of the life and movements found in plants and animals. Without air all of these beings quit growing and moving. Other living and moving beings also get their capacity for animation from air. Reichard notes that "the mountains . . . have the power of motion, given them by the Winds" (1950a:21). Sound, of course, moves by means of air, and this is also true of light (1950a:256). Many of my Navajo friends have pointed out to me that water is also formed in and moved by air. They say water is formed in the clouds which are moved by the winds, and that the water comes to earth by means of the air. They say air is also used to move various fluids by pumping and siphoning. Navajos also say that air exists in water, and that is why fish and other water dwelling creatures, including some plants, are able to live in water. So the source of the apparent capacity of water to move is ultimately found in air.

On some occasions I have queried my intellectual friends among the Navajo concerning the apparent fact that food is really the source of our energy and strength to move, and that without food we would lose our capacity to move. They always agree to that proposition but often point out that there would be no food without air, and that it is air which allows the plants and animals, on which we rely for food, to live and to grow.

The Navajos are also quick to point out that the powerful agent, fire, from which they derive both heat and cooking, is totally dependent on air. Like animals and plants, fires die without air. In mythology fires are described as breathing in air and breathing out smoke, which is a transformed kind of air that bears a resemblance to speech. A similar process occurs when human beings smoke tobacco, which Navajos think of as a form of speech and communication. This attitude toward smoking is true not only for Navajos but for most Native Americans. The food of the fire is the substance, usually wood, which it transforms or digests. The transformation, however, is impossible without air.

Nearly all of the propositions that have been presented above are found in the Navajo story of creation; and I, therefore, think it worthwhile to quote at length from the Navajo story of creation:

The First World

These stories were told to Sandoval, Hastin Tlo'tsi hee, by his grandmother, Esdzan Hosh kige. Her ancestor was Esdzan at a', the medicine woman who had the Calendar Stone in her keeping. Here are the stories of the Four Worlds that had no sun, and of the Fifth, the world we live in, which some call the Changeable World.

The First World, Ni'hodilqil, was black as black wool. It had four corners, and over these appeared four clouds.

These four clouds contained within themselves the elements of the First World. They were in color, black, white, blue, and yellow.

The Black Cloud represented the Female Being or Substance. For as a child sleeps when being nursed, so life slept in the darkness of the Female Being. The White Cloud represented the Male Being or Substance. He was the Dawn, the Light-Which-Awakens, of the First World.

In the East, at the place where the Black Cloud and the White Cloud met, First Man, Atse'hastqin, was formed; and with him was formed the white corn, perfect in shape, with kernels covering the whole ear. Dohonot i'ni is the name of this first seed corn, and it is also the name of the place where the Black Cloud and the White Cloud met.

The First World was small in size, a floating island in mist or water. On it there grew one tree, a pine tree, which was later brought to the present world for firewood.

Man was not, however, in his present form. The conception was of a male and a female being who were to become man and woman. The creatures of the First World are thought of as the Mist People; they had no definite form, but were to change to men, beasts, birds, and reptiles of this world.

Now on the western side of the First World, in a place that later was to become the Land of Sunset, there appeared the Blue Cloud, and opposite it there appeared the Yellow Cloud. Where they came together First Woman was formed, and with her the yellow corn. This ear of corn was also perfect. With First Woman there came the white shell and the turquoise and the yucca.

First Man stood on the eastern side of the First World. He represented the Dawn, and was the Life Giver. First Woman stood opposite in the West. She represented Darkness and Death.

First Man burned a crystal for a fire. The crystal belonged to the male and was the symbol of the mind and of clear seeing. When First Man burned it, it was the mind's awakening. First Woman burned her turquoise for a fire. They saw each other's lights in the distance. When the Black Cloud and the White Cloud rose higher in the sky First Man set out to find the turquoise light. He went twice without success, and again a third time; then he broke a forked branch from his tree, and, looking through the fork, he marked the place where the light burned. And the fourth time he walked to it and found smoke coming from a home.

"Here is the home I could not find," First Man said.

First Woman answered: "Oh, it is you. I saw you walking around and I wondered why you did not come."

Again the same thing happened when the Blue Cloud and the Yellow Cloud rose higher in the sky. First Woman saw a light and she went out to find it. Three times she was unsuccessful, but the fourth time she saw the smoke and she found the home of First Man.

"I wondered what this thing could be," she said.

"I saw you walking and I wondered why you did not come to me," First Man answered.

First Woman saw that First Man had a crystal for a fire, and she saw that it was stronger than her turquoise fire. And as she was thinking, First Man spoke to her. "Why do you not come with your fire and we will live together." The woman agreed to this. So instead of the man going to the woman, as is the custom now, the woman went to the man (O'Bryan, 1956:1–3).

There are several significant points to be drawn from this text. The essential elements from which life forms evolved were four kinds of clouds or gases, differentiated by their color. In the Navajo version the verb stem does not specify that these four elements were clouds but only indicates that they were in a gaseous state. Where the white gas and the black gas conjoined, the first form of life appeared and contained within itself the male principle, and was called First Man. Likewise, the yellow and blue gases conjoined, and another form of life came into being, containing within itself the female principle, and was called First Woman. It was from these primordial unions that the earth surface people and other creatures of the fifth world eventually evolved. Although the text refers to the original beings of the first world as mist people, my intellectual friends have always maintained that they were *nitch'i dine'é* 'air people', who evolved in the air where water was undergoing vaporization and were transparent except for their color.

Fire is used here as an appealing and an appropriate metaphor. If we think of the original beings as forms of air, then their association or identification with fire becomes more clear. They, as sources of air, maintain their fires; the smoke signals from their fires are associated with their forms of speech and communication. They invoke each other to come by means of their smoke signals. In the version recorded by Goddard (1933:127) which is more carefully translated, we find that it is when the colored smoke gets absorbed into the white or transparent atmosphere that they lose sight of it and forget its direction. It is only after they acquire a tool—a pointing stick—to decipher the message and keep it in focus that communication and eventual union are made possible. This story becomes even more revealing of the beauty and logic of Navajo thought when we remember that the explicit name of this first world is *saad ła'í* 'first language'. This illustrates how significant the Navajos feel that language was in both the biological and cultural evolution of man; and language, it should be remembered, is made possible by the projection of symbols into the air, both in its crude form found in the first world and in its very sophisticated form found in the present fifth world.

Knowledge is also an inherent possession of air. In Navajo mythology wind is the supreme mentor or informer, continually imparting information to the various beings to give them a guide for their actions (Reichard, 1950a:72, 134, 149, 499). Reichard notes the following:

> Mentors are few and, like the gods, each may be a different aspect of a single idea. Those most commonly mentioned in my material are Big Fly and Wind. They are said to "sit on the ear" of a person who needs instruction and to whisper answers to questions or forecast the future. . . . Big Fly, when a daytime mentor, may be symbolized as Wind's Child. . . . Mentors are described as ever present, although invisible (1950a:64).

Having established the association of air with element, symbol, knowledge and language, it is now appropriate to connect these propositions with thought and speech, and thereby get a better view as to why the Navajo attribute so much power to thought and speech. Knowledge is associated with one's breath, which, of course, is associated with one's air soul and one's life and movement (Haile, 1943:66). One of Haile's informants offered the following explanation:

> White wind gave his daughter and her son part of his breath, just as a man teaches his son or his sister's son prayers and songs and they become his; or as a father or mother may give their daughter and son advice and instruction. . . . He became their soul without diminishing himself, and gave them movement and life (1943:74).

Elsewhere Haile notes that the Navajo readily admits that "the wind soul is the means 'by which he has life, movement, speech, dream, and thought' " (1943:83).

No one is considered normal or whole unless his -gáál 'power of motion' is unimpaired. Reichard notes that:

> Besides motion a person's sound is also a faculty and this is demonstrated time and again by words like 'sound power'

(-*i·né·'*), speech and verbs which indicate uttering sound of a general or specific nature. . . . It is important to note in this connection that ritualistically sound, speech, breath, and motion are so closely related that blowing into the ears or shouting loudly into a deaf person's ear is believed to restore his breath or his speech (1944:51).

Although the Navajo have many closely related terms for breath, breathing, sound, speech, and so on, the most significant of these terms is *ájí* which Reichard translates:

'life and power of a being as well as its breath, that which keeps him powerful, that which a being acquires through ritual'. It also means namesake, that which is secured by identification. This word is used in the ritualistic phrase 'breathing in' or 'inhaling' (*yíjí yidjíj*), which designates an act signifying the acceptance by the patient of all that has been done for him in the ceremony (1944:51–52).

Recalling that both knowledge and animation are inherent to air and that the "in-standing air soul" is what allows one to think and plan for the future, it is evident that air is what makes thought possible. Only beings or entities which breathe may think. The connection between thought and speech has already been established, and the fact that it is air that makes speech possible needs no elaboration. There are, however, a few less obvious aspects of this process which should be elaborated.

To the Navajo, sound is air in motion, and speech is highly refined and patterned air in motion. To put sound in patterned motion, one must control air. Air contains the supreme power of motion in the universe and the ultimate source of all knowledge. To control air is a process by which man participates in the omnipotence and omniscience of air. Thus the speech act is the ultimate act of knowledge and power, and by speaking properly and appropriately one can control and compel the behavior and power of the gods. This is the ontological and rational basis of the compulsive power of speech.

Air is not only omnipotent and omniscient, it is also omnipre:
ent. It connects, encircles, and fills the whole world. All animate
beings depend on it—live by it, move by it, think by it, and speak
by it. Because it is the means of thought and speech, it knows all
thoughts and actions. It can carry messages to the inner forms of
all things. Because it is the source of all life and motion, it is the
ultimate source of *hózhǫ́*. To control air and to speak and sing the
order, harmony, and beauty of *hózhǫ́* is to make contact with the
ultimate source of life and restore it to the ideal condition of
hózhǫ́. After a person has projected *hózhǫ́* into the air through
ritual form, he then, at the conclusion of the ritual, breathes that
hózhǫ́ back into himself and makes himself a part of the order,
harmony, and beauty he has projected onto the world through
the ritual mediums of speech and song.

The *diyin dine'é* are the inner forms of various natural phenomena in this world. To control these phenomena one must control
their inner forms. The inner forms get their knowledge and
power from the air, and so it is through the air that an earth
surface person can control the *diyin dine'é*. By controlling the *diyin
dine'é,* one can control the natural phenomena whose inner forms
they constitute.

Control of a particular *diyin dine'é* is accomplished by knowledge
of his or her symbols (particularly his or her name), knowledge of
his or her offering, and knowledge of the smells, sights, and sounds
which attract, please, and compel him or her. The correct songs,
prayers, and symbols are irresistible and compulsive. A Navajo
does not supplicate or worship his gods; he identifies himself with
them and both controls their power and incorporates their power
within himself. To control the gods, he must raise himself above
them; for if he lowered himself below them, why should they identify themselves with him? He does not say "not my will, but thine,
be done"; he says "my will be done." And because his will is thrust
into and imposed upon the omnipotent, omniscient, and omnipres-
ent air in which the god himself lives, thinks, speaks, and acts, both
the singer's and the speaker's will is done.

Reichard once observed that "Navajo dogma connects all things, natural and experienced, from man's skeleton to universal destiny, which encompasses even inconceivable space, in a closely interlocked unity which omits nothing, no matter how small or how stupendous" (1943:360). It is air which is the source and sustainer of all things. It is air which connects all things and unites all things into the universal ideal described by the words *sǫ'ah naagháii bik'eh hózhǫ́*. Man participates in this beauty, harmony, and order—this fountain of life, power, and knowledge—through his breath, his thoughts, and his speech. It is language through which man harmonizes with the blessedness of his environment, and through which he restores this blessedness when it has been disrupted. Without language man is impotent, ignorant, isolated, and static. He is, in fact, an inactive part of a cosmos in which he cannot find any meaning for his being. With language man is an active, creative, and powerful part of his universe. Through language, the meaning that he finds in his being and that he creates and expresses through his being is fused with the omniscience, omnipotence, and omnipresence of air, the source of all life, beauty, and harmony.

CHAPTER 3
Classifying the World through Language

I. CLASSIFYING INTERACTION

Recently Kenneth Hale (1973) brought to light a fascinating aspect of Navajo syntax, which is very significantly related to Navajo conceptions of the way in which entities in the Navajo world interact. Hale refers to this feature of Navajo syntax as a rule of subject-object inversion. From a surface level point of view, the rule appears to cause the object of the sentence to become the subject and the subject of the sentence to become the object. The rule seems to apply only to transitive sentences in which two third persons are interacting. Let me illustrate this by starting with what Hale assumes is a normal or regular pattern for transitive sentences:

> (1) *Łį́į́'* *dzaanééz* *yiztał*
>   (horse) (mule) (it-it-kicked)

The sentence above translates into English as 'the horse kicked the mule'. A Navajo verb includes both object and subject pronouns as well as the verb stem which denotes the action performed. With regard to the position of these elements in the verb, the object always comes before the subject and the subject always precedes the stem. In the sentences above, the *yi* (it) refers to the object (the mule). When the object pronoun *bi* 'it' replaces the object pronoun *yi* 'it', the result appears to be an inversion of subject and object when the sentence is freely translated into English.

> (2) *Łį́į́'* *dzaanééz* *biztał*
>   (horse) (mule) (it-it-kicked)

63

The free translation of sentence (2), which Hale and everyone else has assumed to be correct, is 'the horse was kicked by the mule'. In this case, then, it is the mule that did the kicking and the horse that got kicked. The syntactical construction of both sentences is the same, but the insertion of the *bi* object pronoun for the *yi* object pronoun appears to have inverted the origin and direction of the action. Although I will later disagree with the translations of these sentences which have heretofore been assumed, I do not question the fact that it is the mule which got kicked in sentence (1) and that it is the horse which got kicked in sentence (2). What I do question is the assumption that because the horse got kicked it is necessarily the object of sentence two. Moreover, I do not assume that the horse which got kicked is the one which in the final or ultimate sense is the "acted upon," or that the mule which did the kicking is the primary "actor" of the sentence. Having stated this suspicion about what appears on the surface of things to be indubitable, I will proceed for awhile on the assumption that the *bi* form does cause an inversion of subject and object, and will leave a discussion of the accuracy of this assumption until later.

The relationship of this rule of subject-object inversion to Navajo world view is not evident from the two sentences provided above. However, when we change the mule to a man, something strange seems to occur. We find that the sentence 'the man kicked the horse'

(3)   *Hastiin*   *łį́į́'*   *yiztał*
       (man)   (horse)   (it-it-kicked)

is acceptable, but that the sentence 'the horse was kicked by the man'

(4)   *Łį́į́'*   *hastiin*   *biztał*
       (horse)   (man)   (it-it-kicked)

is unacceptable. Sentence (4) is not just poor grammar; it is an impossibility in the Navajo world.

By interposing the object pronouns *bi* and *yi*, two more sentences become grammatically possible. One is the sentence 'the man was kicked by the horse'

| (5) | *Hastiin* | *łįį'* | *biztał* |
| | (man) | (horse) | (it-it-kicked) |

which is acceptable; the other is the sentence 'the horse kicked the man'

| (6) | *Łįį'* | *hastiin* | *yiztał* |
| | (horse) | (man) | (it-it-kicked) |

which is grammatically regular but culturally unacceptable. In the Navajo view of the world, it is absurd to think that a horse could kick a man. Why, we ask from our Western frame of reference, is it absurd to think that a horse could kick a man?

Lest we think that this rule relates only to horses, mules, and men, additional examples are provided. The sentence 'the girl drank the water'

| (7) | *At'ééd* | *tó* | *yoodlą́ą́'* |
| | (girl) | (water) | (it-it-drank) |

is acceptable, but the sentence 'the water was drunk by the girl'

| (8) | *Tó* | *at'ééd* | *boodlą́ą́'* |
| | (water) | (girl) | (it-it-drank) |

is unacceptable and absurd in the Navajo view of the world. One of the interesting aspects of the absurdity that the Navajo see in sentences (4), (6), and (8) is that this absurdity varies in degree. Sentence (8) is much more absurd than sentence (6), but sentence (6) is only slightly more absurd than sentence (4). In exploring this matter further we find that 'the girl can be drowned (killed) by the water'

| (9) | *At'ééd* | *tó* | *biisxí* |
| | (girl) | (water) | (it-it-killed) |

but that the water cannot drown (kill) the girl.

(10)	*Tó*	*at'ééd*	*yiyiisxį*
	(water)	(girl)	(it-it-killed)

Similar peculiarities exist when two inanimate objects act upon each other. Thus the sentence 'the rock rolled upon the tree'

(11)	*Tsé*	*t'iis*	*yik'ich'inímááz*
	(rock)	(tree)	(it-upon-horizontally-it-rolled)

is acceptable, but the sentence 'the tree was rolled upon by the rock'

(12)	*T'iis*	*tsé*	*bik'ich'inímááz*
	(tree)	(rock)	(it-upon-horizontally-it-rolled)

is unacceptable. It is, in fact, an event that, strictly speaking, could not have occurred. Moreover, while the sentence 'the tree fell upon the rock'

(13)	*T'iis*	*tsé*	*yik'iikééz*
	(tree)	(rock)	(it-upon-it-fell)

is acceptable, the sentence 'the rock was fallen upon by the tree'

(14)	*Tsé*	*t'iis*	*bik'iikééz*
	(rock)	(tree)	(it-upon-it-fell)

is unacceptable.

Hale once thought the rule involved the ranking of nouns, and that the higher ranking nouns always had to come first in any sentence (1973:304). Sentences (11) to (14) seem to prove that to be wrong, because in sentence (11) the "rock" is allowed to precede the "tree" but not in sentence (14). Likewise, the "tree" is allowed to precede the "rock" in sentence (13) but not in sentence (12).

It is rather evident from this discussion that we need some nonlinguistic data or information in order to interpret these rather unusual linguistic patterns properly. They are not generated by a set of operations at the deep structural level of Navajo grammar; they are generated by a set of cultural rules which are

ultimately derived from more fundamental metaphysical propositions which the Navajo take to be axiomatic.

Taking a cultural approach to the explanation of this pattern in
Navajo syntax, some years ago I asked my wife why it was so
absurd to say *tó at'ééd boodlą́ą́'* 'the water was drunk by the girl'.
She thought long and hard about this matter, unable to see why it
was not absurd to me. Finally, she said, "The sentence attributes
more intelligence to the water than it does to the girl, and anyone
[even you—was the implication] ought to know that human beings
are smarter than water." Therein I had a lead to solve this riddle,
but I was not sure what to make of it. She went on to say that the
water does not think, so how could it have the girl drink it. But, I
insisted, the water was not acting or thinking, it just got drunk.
She countered by saying that the way I had constructed the sentence made it appear that the water was the cause of the drinking
action, not the girl.

From the discussion above I later surmised that maybe the sentence should be translated 'the water caused the girl to drink it'. I
tried this translation out on several Navajos who knew English.
They said it was much closer to the Navajo meaning of the sentence than 'the water was drunk by the girl' but they were still a
little uncomfortable with it. After some further thought and discussion, we came up with the translation 'the water let the girl
drink it'. Therein we had captured in English not just the covert
meaning of the Navajo sentence but the overt absurdity that the
meaning expressed.

From the insights gained from the conversations mentioned
above, it soon dawned on me that this whole set of behaviors
relating to the supposed rule of subject-object inversion was really
based on some of the same metaphysical notions that I had found
in Navajo ritual behavior. It deals with the phenomena of movement and action, referring particularly to who can control whom,
or who can act upon whom. Let us reconsider some of our examples in this new light.

In sentence (1) we find that the horse can kick the mule. In
sentence (2) we find that the horse can let the mule kick it. What

sentence (2) suggests is that the horse by its own acquiescence or inadvertence permitted, maybe even encouraged, the mule to kick it. Such a statement describes a much different event than the simple sentence *dzaanééz łį́į́' yiztał* 'the mule kicked the horse' which attributes both the origin and the control of the action to the mule.

Sentences (3) through (6) make even more sense in this new light. Sentence (3) is clearly all right because the man can properly act upon and control the horse. Sentence (4) is unacceptable because it says 'the horse let the man kick it', which seems to attribute more intelligence to the horse than it does to the man. The man, in the Navajo view of the world, is more intelligent than the horse and can control and act upon the horse without asking for or getting the horse's consent. There is also an implication in this sentence that the horse is in control of the man, and that it encourages, if not compels, the man to kick it. Such notions about the relationship between horses and men seem absurd to the Navajo, and to speak in that way leaves one open to the suspicion of idiocy or insanity. But these notions are nowhere near as absurd as the notion that 'the water let (or caused) the girl drink it'. The difference is that the gap in intelligence (capacity for thought) and capacity for action and control is much wider between human beings and water than it is between human beings and horses.

Sentence (5) should be translated 'the man let the horse kick him'. Here the assumption is that the man with greater intelligence could have, by using his mental powers and resources, prevented the horse from kicking him. Nevertheless, through acquiescence or inadvertence, the man at least consented and may have even encouraged or caused the horse to kick him. This sentence is acceptable because the man remains the primary source and controller of the action.

Sentence (6) is absurd because it claims that the horse can both decide to kick the man and accomplish the feat without the man's consent, either openly provided or inadvertently given. It means that the horse was intellectually dominating the man and had the man under its control, with the man unable to resist. Again such notions about the relationship between horses and men seem absurd to the Navajo. Sentences (9) and (10) make a similar point as they tell us (9) the girl can let the water kill her, but (10) the water cannot take it upon itself to kill the girl. The water does not possess intent or will and thus cannot control or act upon the girl.

Sentences (11) through (14) reveal that movement and action are part of the considerations that decide who can control or act upon whom. In sentence (11) the rock hits the tree. The rock in this case is superior to the tree because of its locomotion. The tree, being static and lacking in intelligence, cannot resist. Therefore, sentence (12) is absurd because it says 'the tree let the rock hit it'. The tree did not have the capacity to resist in the first place, so how could it give consent? The rock by the power of its locomotion was superior to the tree and thus did not need the acquiescence of the tree to act upon it.

Sentences (13) and (14) illustrate the same points found in sentences (11) and (12). This time, however, it is the tree that is in motion and the rock which is static. Sentence (14) is absurd because static entities cannot control or resist falling trees.

Hale has proposed two ways of explaining the nature and application of the *bi* object pronoun which he believes results in an inversion of subject and object. He finds that "there are circumstances in which subject-object inversion is optional, others in which it is obligatory, and still others in which it may not apply" (1973:303). He adds that whether the rule is optional, obligatory, or blocked depends on the inherent qualities of the interacting entities or beings. If we assume that the principal and determining quality of interacting agents is animation as opposed to inanimation, Hale offers the following set of conditions for applying the rule (1973:303):

Subject	Object	Inversion
animate	animate	optional
animate	inanimate	blocked
inanimate	inanimate	blocked
inanimate	animate	obligatory

Because the conditions above leave the application of the rule totally optional with regard to any animate being acting on any other animate being and because in actual usage the rule is obligatory in cases such as that of a dog biting a human being, Hale tends to reject this hypothesis in favor of one which assumes that there is a hierarchy of ranked nouns which determines the conditions when the rule is optional or obligatory. This alternative hypothesis is based on the idea that the "purpose of the rule is to give prominence to, to put in focus, or the like, one or the other of the two noun phrases . . . the rule applies in such a way as to ensure that prominence is given to the higher ranking noun phrase . . . " (1973:304). This alternative hypothesis looks like this:

Subject and Object	*Inversion*
subject and object equal in rank	optional
subject outranks object	blocked
object outranks subject	obligatory

Hale summarizes his attitude toward these two alternative hypotheses as follows:

Although it will not be possible, due to my limited control of this aspect of Navajo grammar, to establish either of the alternatives as more nearly correct, there are considerations which make me think that the ranking hypothesis is superior and, further, that the conditions on inversion cannot be formulated in absolute terms (1973;305).

To follow through on his inclination for the ranking hypothesis, Hale encouraged Mary Helen Creamer, a Navajo whose primary area of study and work is in educational administration, to try to formulate the conditions under which the rules apply and to delineate the ranked categories of Navajo nouns. In an excellent and fascinating paper presented to the annual meeting of the American Anthropological Association in 1971, and later published in

Diné Bizaad Náníl'ííh (Navajo Language Review), Creamer presented the conclusions of her research. She found that Navajo nouns are ranked according to inherent qualities and characteristics that Navajos infer from experience in terms of what they ordinarily expect these entities or beings to do, and that "the characteristics of each being identified by a noun in Navajo appear to be summed up in an inherent 'capacity to act upon' in relation to other beings" (1974:30). She adds that the basic idea on which the ranked categories are constituted and distinguished is that of "who can be expected to be able to act upon whom" (1974:30).

Mary Helen Creamer's research led her to posit the existence of eight ranked groups or categories into one of which all Navajo nouns fall. She maintains that nouns may freely act upon other nouns of equal or lower status but not on nouns of higher status. To prevent nouns of lower status from being the subject of a sentence and occurring first in that sentence, the subject-object inversion rule becomes obligatory (1974:32). She concludes, following Hale, that "the semantic effect of subject-object inversion in this case appears to be quite similar to that of the passive in English" (1974:32). The eight ranked groups she delineates are as follows:

Group 1. Nouns denoting persons
Group 2. Nouns denoting the larger animals and medium-sized animals of special intelligence or relationship to man (such as the dog) and predators
Group 3. Nouns denoting medium sized animals . . .
Group 4. Nouns denoting small sized animals . . .
Group 5. Nouns denoting insects . . .
Group 6. Nouns denoting natural forces
Group 7. Nouns denoting plants and inanimate objects
Group 8. Nouns denoting abstractions such as old age, hunger, disease . . . (1974:33–37).

By Hale's ranking hypothesis, according to which the groups above have been delineated, entities or beings within each group can freely act upon each other, and thus the inversion rule is optional. The inversion rule becomes obligatory when a lower status being acts upon a higher status being, assuring that the higher status noun precedes the lower status noun in the syntax of the sentence. Thus one does not say 'the horse kicked the boy';

(15)	*Łíí'*	*ashkii*	*yiztał*
	(horse)	(boy)	(it-it-kicked)

one says 'the boy was kicked by the horse'.

(16)	*Ashkii*	*łíí'*	*biztał*
	(boy)	(horse)	(it-it-kicked)

Hale concludes from this that sentence (15) is not preferred because it allows a lower status noun to precede a higher status noun. Thus sentence (16) which uses the inversion rule is the preferred sentence because it places the higher status noun (boy) before the lower status noun (horse) (1973:304). I reject this underlying assumption on which Hale's ranking hypothesis is based. Although I do not reject the idea that entities and beings in the Navajo world are ranked according to who can act upon or control whom, I do reject the hypothesis that this usage has anything to do with ensuring that higher status nouns come first in a sentence. My rejection of this assumption is based on both intuitive and empirical grounds, for I cannot see how it corresponds to any of the ways according to which Navajos conceive, describe, or explain the world, and it does not adequately portray the semantic dimensions or implications of the *bi* form, nor does it, in fact, correspond to actual usage.

The use of the *bi* third person object pronoun form does not in fact cause an inversion of subject and object, and what results from its use is not, as Hale assumes, anything very similar to the passive in English. Sentence (15) states that 'the horse kicked the boy'. This sentence is rejected by speakers of Navajo not because the lower status noun precedes the higher status noun, but because in the Navajo conception of the world human beings are more intelligent than horses, and thus horses cannot will and carry out actions against human beings without the action being stimulated or caused by the conscious will of the human being or by his careless, inadvertent behavior. In sentence (16) the boy is the prime mover of the action and also is the recipient of the action; the horse is only the agent or means by which the action is accomplished. The resulting semantic context of the sentence is more like the English reflexive than it is like the English passive. This sentence might better be translated 'the boy had himself kicked by means of the horse'.

The ranking hypothesis does not account for the absurd and humorous nature of many incorrect statements. If it were just a matter of keeping the higher status noun first in the sentence, then the sentence 'the water was drunk by the girl'

(17)	*Tó*	*at'ééd*	*boodlą́ą́'*
	(water)	(girl)	(it-it-drank)

would simply be poor grammar. It is, however, much more than poor grammar; it is humorously absurd, suggesting the likely idiocy of the person who constructed it. Navajos laugh profusely when they hear such a statement. When this sentence is translated into the English passive, we do not see either the humor or the absurdity that the Navajos see in it. If, however, we translate this sentence as 'the water got itself drunk by means of the girl', we get closer to the meaning and absurdity of the sentence. Another better translation would be 'the water let (or caused) the girl drink it'.

The idea that the water could by means of its will, of which it has none, cause or control the behavior of the girl is absolutely absurd to the Navajo, and they find it hard to see why we do not see this same absurdity. If we did not cast this sentence back into one of our categories—the passive—we could more easily appreciate the humor and absurdity of the sentence.

A more empirical reason for rejecting the assumptions on which the ranking hypothesis is based is that they do not account for the data of actual usage. Where two entities of the same status are interacting, the use of the inversion rule is supposed to be optional. But the data of usage show that when two inanimate beings or entities are interacting, the inversion rule is not an option. Recall sentences (11) through (14). The *bi* form is not permitted, but the tree is allowed to precede the rock, and the rock is allowed to precede the tree. The ranking hypothesis about higher status nouns coming first in the sentence gives us no clue as to why the inversion rule is not an option in this case. In this case again, the use of the *bi* form makes the resulting semantic content of the sentences humorous and absurd. The more correct translation of the semantic content of sentence (12) is 'the tree let the rock roll against it'. This attributes to the tree both the power of thought and the capacity to resist or avoid the rolling rock. Viewed in this way, the underlying humor and absurdity of the sentence become clear and unmistakable.

The reason that the *bi* form is not used when two inanimate objects are interacting is that it attributes to them a power to think and a capacity to resist controlling action by another inanimate object. The acting or moving inanimate object gets its power to act upon something by having been animated by some other being or entity; for instance, a man may have rolled the rock into the tree. The static tree has no inherent capacity to think, speak, resist, or avoid the animation of the rock. To use the *bi* form as is done in sentence (12) attributes inherent qualities to the tree which it does not possess, and thus construes a description of an event in the Navajo world which by axiomatic definition could not have occurred.

Further examples of this failure of the ranking hypothesis to account for actual usage would be the sentences 'the water carried off the stick'

(18)	*Tó*	*tsin*	*'ayíìł'éél*
	(water)	(stick)	(away-it-it-carried)

and 'the snow froze the milk'.

(19)	*Yas*	*abe'*	*yistin*
	(snow)	(milk)	(it-it-froze)

Both of these sentences are culturally acceptable, but to alter them by using the inversion rule makes them unacceptable. Thus the sentence 'the stick let the water carry it off'

(20)   *Tsin*   *tó*   *abííł éél*
        (stick)   (water)   (away-it-it-carried)

is absurd, just as is the sentence, 'the milk let (or caused) the snow freeze it'.

(21)   *Abe'*   *yas*   *bistin*
        (milk)   (snow)   (it-it-froze)

Because these are all nouns of approximately the same status, there is no reason or explanation why, according to the ranking hypothesis, sentences (20) and (21) are unacceptable.

Although I disagree with some of the details of her presentation of Navajo categories, I strongly agree with Creamer's statement that the basis of the categories is "summed up in an inherent 'capacity to act upon'," and that "exceptions to these rankings appear to be related to the same common sense ideas of 'who can be expected to be able to act upon whom' " (1974:30). It will be recalled that a large part of Navajo ritual is based on the earth surface people's capacity to control and compel the Holy People through ritual action, song, and prayer. Who can act upon whom or who can control whom is of basic interest and concern to Navajos and is one of the dominant perspectives in the Navajo world view.

The Navajo view of the world is based on two metaphysical premises that are relevant to an interpretation of the phenomenon of subject-object inversion. One of these is a willful and pervasive determinism, and the other is an unbreakable link between the worlds of thought and speech and the worlds of matter and energy. Both of these presuppositions are contradicted or denied in Western metaphysics, and they both, therefore, require some elaboration if we are going to be able to understand how the Navajo interpret and explain the events that occur in their world.

Although there is a deterministic school of thought in philosophy, and scientific methodology assumes a kind of determinism, ours is not a willful determinism. We do not believe all events and conditions are determined by the will or intent of some intelligent being or beings. Scientific determinism projects that events in the world of nature or the world of matter and energy are determined and controlled by natural laws of cause and effect relationships, and they have nothing to do with the mind, will, or intent of any being. Despite this sort of determinism, which some intellectuals in the West adopt to explain some things, a basic and pervasive belief among Westerners is that much of what happens is a result of luck, fortune, or fate. This view is based on the presuppositions of accident, coincidence, and randomness. These metaphysical notions permeate our view of human events and affairs.

In the Navajo view of the world all entities which have the capacity for self-animation are directed and controlled by the power of thought. The power or energy source of all life and animation is located in the air, but the director and controller of all animation is the mind. All movements, events, and conditions are ultimately controlled by the thought of one or more beings. Although entities without the capacity to think have the ability to move, their movements are caused and controlled by some being who has the power to think. The world view resulting from these metaphysical presuppositions is an all-pervasive determinism in which all matter and energy, events and conditions are ultimately controlled by the thought and will of intelligent or thinking beings. What happens at any given moment in the Navajo world is determined by who can control what or who can control whom. A particular being's capacity to control other beings and things is based on his capacity to think and his capacity to project his thoughts or will onto reality.

Since this section is concerned with an analysis of inversion, I might as well add another characteristically Navajo inversion. Reichard tells us the following:

One of the outstanding aspects of Navajo dogma is its essential duality, but once having said this, we are more apt to be misled than enlightened, for we popularly consider that good is good and bad is bad. . . . It is therefore difficult to comprehend that in the Navajo interpretation of duality good *is* evil and evil is good (1944:5).

The sum total of this inverted duality is neutrality. Things and beings, events and conditions, processes and powers are neither good nor evil, or are potentially both good and evil. In the beginning matter existed in a neutral, unordered, and unformed condition. Thought and speech transformed matter into an ordered and formed condition. Evil came into the world when things went out of control and became disordered. Good came into the world when evil yielded to the controlling power of ritual, power which is contained in its ordered ways of thinking, speaking, and acting. Evil keeps coming into the world when things get out of control and good thus becomes evil; then good returns to the world when, under control, evil becomes good. To quote Reichard (1943:5) again, "the difference between the two [good and evil] is in the presence or absence of control, which in its turn ultimately depends upon . . . ritual. . . . "

As pointed out earlier, the crucial question in Navajo determinism is who can control what or who can control whom. This is determined primarily by the level of one's intelligence and, to a lesser extent, by the potency of one's animation. Thus we might roughly conclude that in Navajo physics C(control) = M(mass) $\times$ I^2(intelligence). Beings and entities in the Navajo world are categorized and ranked according to a scale based on who can control whom. Beings of lower intelligence cannot control or act upon beings of higher intelligence, unless the beings of higher intelligence willfully or inadvertently yield to the control of beings of lower intelligence.

My own attempt to represent the ways in which Navajos categorize the world based on the perspective discussed above is found in figure 4. This representation claims that the basic distinction is, as Hale first presented and later rejected, between animate and inanimate. Animate beings are clearly assumed to be able to control inanimate entities because animation necessarily involves some degree of intelligence and because auto-locomotion is the most visible demonstration of potency. Because, as we discovered in chapter 2, all being or existence is divided up into two dimensions or natures, and because overwhelming emphasis is given to the active over the static, it is also a rather obvious conclusion that active beings have a greater capacity to control static beings than vice versa.

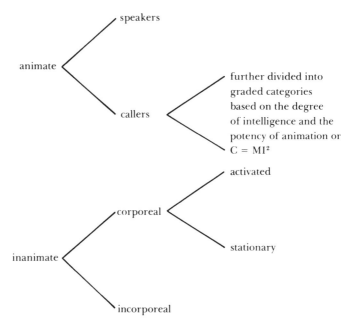

Fig. 4. Navajo Classification of Control

Inanimate entities are divided into two types: (1) those with material, corporeal existence, such as rocks, trees, jewels, metals, and so on; and (2) abstractions without a material or corporeal existence, such as hunger, thirst, ideas, emotions, and so on. To illustrate this distinction, a Navajo would not say "hunger (or starvation) killed the man" or "thirst killed the tree"; he would say "the man allowed himself to die as a result of hunger" or "the tree caused itself to die by means of thirst." If the power to control (C) is measured by mass (M) times intelligence squared (I^2), then incorporeal abstractions without either mass or intelligence would be the least potent of all things in the universe.

Animate beings are divided into two categories: speakers and callers. Speakers are those capable of speaking a language, and callers are those just capable of calling, crying, howling, barking, humming, and so on. Father Berard Haile notes the following:

> A human being, therefore, could be characterized by the generic term: *yáłti'i* 'one who speaks', as opposed to: *do yáłti'i* 'non-speaker', primarily referring to plants and animals. . . . But animals also have souls, because they breathe, walk, and give their calls: *'ání*, 'it gives a call', as opposed to *yáłti'* he 'speaks' (1943:76–77).

The classification described above also corresponds with the fact that human babies who cannot speak but can call and cry are not classified as equal to human beings who have acquired the art of speaking. Thus it is unacceptable to say 'the baby kicked the man';

Awéé'	*hastiin*	*yiztał*
(baby)	(man)	(it-it-kicked)

one must say 'the man let the baby kick him'.

Hastiin	*awéé'*	*biztał*
(man)	(baby)	(it-it-kicked)

However, one can say 'the baby kicked the horse',

Awéé'	*łį́į́'*	*yiztał*

and one can also say 'the horse kicked the baby'.

Łíí'   *awéé'*   *yiztał*

These sentences make it clear that the human baby who can only call and cry is considered to be approximately equal to animals who can only call and cry. Human beings who are deaf and dumb are also classified with the animals according to classifications based on the perspective of who can control whom. Here again we see the tremendous emphasis Navajos place on language as a means of controlling the universe. It is through language that man acquires human status. It is through language that man acquires the capacity to control the Holy People, the inner forms of powerful natural forces and entities that control and maintain the operation of the fifth world. Without language man is greatly reduced in stature, and his control of the world about him is greatly impaired. He becomes the acted upon rather than the actor, the created rather than the creator, the object rather than the subject.

Animate but nonspeaking beings are further differentiated according to something approaching or approximating the equation $C = M \times I^2$. It is quite clear to Navajos that bears are more intelligent and more potent than mice but it is not so clear as to whether bears are more intelligent than dogs, or whether mice are more intelligent and potent than chipmunks. Creamer tells us that a bee can sting a spider but not a mouse; the mouse can only let itself be stung by the bee (1974:36). A cat can bite a mouse, but a cat can only let itself be bitten by a mouse. A dog, however, can bite a cat and a cat can bite a dog.

Cases of interaction between animate but nonspeaking beings are not always clearly and precisely defined. There is no dispute about the idea of a horse acting upon a cat, but some people would dispute the idea of a cat acting upon a horse. Hale also mentions this apparent phenomenon:

In the clearest cases, e.g., where the logical subject and logical object are noticeably unequal in rank, or where they are unquestionably equal, speakers of Navajo can be rather firm in their judgments about acceptability. . . . But there are areas where judgments are not so firm, areas where it is perhaps more appropriate to speak of relative acceptability (1973:306).

Probably the best way to conceptualize this area of animate but nonspeaking beings is to consider it to be a continuum rather than a set of tightly bound groups or categories.

Inanimate entities are differentiated by whether they have been activated or whether they are in a static or stationary position. Thus "the rock rolls against the tree" but "the tree falls upon the rock." If they both have been activated (put in motion), then the one whose animation is the most potent is considered to have the capacity to act upon or control the one with the least potent animation.

Earlier it was shown how many forms of ritual action and behavior become intelligible and rational when the underlying metaphysical propositions on which they are based are known and understood. Here we find that those same propositions about static and active, potency of activity and potency of thought and speech make comprehensible linguistic usage and speech behavior that on their surface defy adequate explanation. These underlying and axiomatic assumptions about the nature and operation of reality also make Navajo classifications of the universe more logical and sensible, and through an appreciation and understanding of the logical ordering of their world we can also see absurdity where they see absurdity and humor where they see humor. In this way we can learn not only to converse with them, but also to laugh with them.

II. CLASSIFYING AFFECTIVE ACTION

In chapters 1 and 2 and in the preceding section of this chapter, attention was focused on the concept of control and on the means

ı certain beings are able to control other beings and en-
lthough the concept of control is extremely important in
anding the nature of ritual language and in understanding the dimensions of interaction between different kinds of beings and entities, the attribute or capacity to control other beings
is appropriately used only when affective and harmonious relationships are not possible and where it is necessary for one's life
and well-being to control other beings.

In Navajo ritual the concept of control applies mainly to the
Diyink'ehgo ("Holyway") and *Hóchxǫ'jí* ("Evilway") rites. In the
Holyway rites, *Diyin Dine'é* ("Holy People") who are potentially
dangerous or malevolent must be controlled and compelled to use
their power for man's benefit. In the Evilway rites, the evil and
harmful powers of malevolent Holy People must be controlled
and exorcised. However, in the *Hózhǫ́ǫ́jí* ("Blessingway") rites, affective and harmonious identification with benevolent Holy
People is the standard pattern of ritual action. Here the ideals of
k'é solidarity (love, kindness, and cooperation) are always invoked
to emphasize the affective bond between the patient and the Holy
Person or People with whom he is being identified.

Because control is something one utilizes only in relating to
malevolent or potentially malevolent beings with whom an affective and harmonious relationship is impossible, Navajos abhor the
idea or practice of controlling other beings in the normal course
of everyday life. This attitude is most poignantly felt in relationship to other Navajos, but it also extends to animals and plants as
well. Only real and immediate need justifies the killing of an animal or the cutting down of a tree. On such occasions a prayer is
said to the plant or animal, explaining one's need and asking the
pardon or indulgence of the plant or the animal. Reichard observed this respectful attitude toward plant life:

> The Navaho have a sentimental attitude toward plants,
> which they treat with incredible respect.... To pick them
> without taking them into ritual, to let them wither as cut
> flowers is quite out of order, even dangerous, there being no

aesthetic compensation for the fear such sacrilege may engender (1950a:22, 144).

With regard to Navajo attitudes toward the unnecessary taking of animal life, Downs notes the following:

> Many observers of the Navajo have commented that in large part their resentment of the stock reduction program was due to the government's allowing thousands of sheep to die in holding pens or en route to the railroads. Such behavior, perfectly understandable in white economic terms, was viewed as utter barbarism by the Navajo and is still spoken of in Piñon (1964:92–93).

Navajos believe that each person should have the right to speak and act as he pleases, so long as his intentions are not malevolent or his actions harmful to others. Desirable and ethical behavior on the part of others is hoped for and even expected, but it is never demanded or required. Coercion and control are always deplored in interpersonal and intra-group relations. Downs described this attitude as a belief in the "inviolability of the individual." He further discusses some of the social implications of this belief:

> Despite close and absolutely essential familial ties, the Navajo remain highly individualistic people. Their primary social premise might be said to be that no person has the right to speak for or to direct the actions of another (1964:69).

In intra-group relations no individual, regardless of position or status, has the right to impose his will on the group. Likewise, the group does not have the right to impose its will on the individual. Unanimity is the only acceptable basis of collective action. Although a system of majority rule has been imposed on the Navajos for half a century, the extent to which the principle of unanimity continues to pervade almost all social and political deliberations is amazing. In searching for a key to the Navajo social system, Shepardson and Hammond came upon the phrase *bílá* 'it's up to him', which is heard so frequently among the Navajo. They note that "just as this is a Navajo informant's regular response to questions about expected behavior, so it is his view of the society's patterned relations" (1970:241).

This reluctance to avoid even the slightest appearance of attempting to speak for or control the actions of others is also significantly marked or expressed in Navajo grammar and linguistic behavior. A Navajo never addresses another person by name or speaks the name of another person when he is present. Names are one of the principal means by which potentially malevolent Holy People are controlled and commanded. Beyond this practice of not using names in address, there is a separate person (called the Navajo fourth person by Hale and others) in the conjugations of all verbs which is primarily used in reference to states and actions of people who are in the presence or within hearing distance of the speaker. The Navajo fourth person is also used when speaking about something in the hypothetical sense. It has an impersonal, indirect, and nonspecific connotation, and thus is politely used when talking about someone in the presence of the speaker. The impersonality and indirectness of this fourth person permits the speaker to avoid any appearance or implication that he is trying to speak for or control the actions of another person. By using the fourth person, the speaker avoids any criticism of his own intentions and any offense to the person of whom he is speaking.

Whereas control and compulsion through the power of thought and speech are the principal modes of behavior toward dangerous things and malevolent or potentially malevolent beings, *k'é* is the principal mode or pattern of relationship towards all other beings. The Navajo term *k'é* is a preverbal element which refers to affective action and solidarity, encompassing such concepts as love, compassion, kindness, friendliness, generosity, and peacefulness. *K'é náhásdlį́į́'* refers to the restoration of the condition of *k'é,* and is appropriately used whenever any conflict or disharmony has been resolved. *K'é nisin* means 'I think, have my mind on, or my intent is governed by the affective ideals of *k'é*'.

The affective ideals expressed by the term *k'é* derive from the Navajo conception of reproduction. In the Navajo world reproduction involves two kinds of affective action: (1) sexual intercourse and (2) the giving and sustaining of life. The former is found in the husband-wife bond, and is characterized by exchange or reciprocity; the latter is found in the mother-child bond and is characterized by the giving of life and the sustaining of life through sharing items of sustenance. It is the mother who is the focal point of both of these kinds of affective action. The husband-wife bond involves what might be called conjugal or affinal solidarity. The mother-child bond involves what might be called cognatic or kinship solidarity. The giving of life and the sharing of sustenance is considered to be the most powerful, the most intense, and the most enduring of these two bonds, and is considered to be the ideal pattern or code for all social interaction. Even affinal relationships are subsumed under the code or rubric of kinship, for affinal terms are rarely used in address because affines usually prefer to use kin terms and think of themselves as kinsmen.

The mother-child bond is characterized by two kinds of closely associated affective action. A speaker of Navajo frequently compares *shimá éí shishchį* 'my mother gave me birth' or literally 'my mother caused me to be born' with *shimá éí shineesá* 'my mother gave me growth' or literally 'my mother caused me to grow'. Thus we might define the mother-child bond in terms of the reproduction and sustenance of life, expressed in the affective actions of giving birth and sharing sustenance.

It is important to recognize that Navajo relations of kinship are symbolized in and defined by actions and not substances. It is the *act* of giving birth and the *act* of sharing sustenance that establish and express bonds of kinship. Although Navajos believe or will acknowledge that through sexual intercourse and birth some kind of common substance is shared, their culture attaches no meaning in terms of affective solidarity to this alleged common substance. Navajos never mention common substance in discussing, discovering, or invoking kinship ties and norms. Kinship is discussed in terms of the *acts* of giving life and sharing sustenance.

To many the distinction between birth as an act and birth as a process through which common substance is shared may seem very slight and almost pointless. It can, however, be an extremely important distinction. Because American and European cultural beliefs about kinship can only be realized through common substance, true or real kinship exists only between those related by common substance. Any extension of kinship terms to something or someone who does not share common substance is called a metaphor, or is qualified by terms such as step-father, foster parent, parent-in-law, or adopted child. Many anthropologists have transported their own cultural definitions to the cultures they have studied, and in the process have considered those who were real kinsmen by local cultural definitions to be quasi-kinsmen or fictive kinsmen, and have attributed these declarations of kinship to metaphorical uses of the kinship idiom.

Sometimes when other peoples are speaking literally, we say they are speaking metaphorically because their statements do not make literal or logical sense from our vantage point in our world. At other times when they are speaking metaphorically, we think they are speaking literally and we conclude either that we do not understand their logic or that they are illogical in their thinking. A very deep and broad understanding of a people's world is required to be able to discern when they are speaking literally or logically and when they are speaking metaphorically or analogically. But this kind of careful discernment is exactly what we have to be able to do if we are to engage ourselves in what has been called thick description; that is, sorting winks from twitches and real winks from mimicked ones (Geertz, 1973:16).

It may well be that to some degree or in at least one sense all real winks are mimicked and that mimicked ones are in some sense real. People speak in degrees and dimensions of literalness. The meanings of native statements often carry many senses— some literal, some metaphorical, and some in between—and are often based on multiple assumptions about the nature of reality— some logical, some analogical, and some in between.

Most people are also capable of constructing humorous statements that are literal enough to be funny but not false enough to be ridiculous. The creation, discernment, and appreciation of truly humorous statements requires a very delicate and sensitive handling of multiple meanings and senses. Because of this very delicate handling and mixing of meanings and senses, skillfully managed by the humorist, few anthropologists really learn to understand and appreciate native humor and even fewer are able intentionally to create humorous statements, although most have no difficulty in doing so unintentionally.

Lying is also part of the behavioral repertoire of most peoples. Lying—at least successful lying, where one's statement is indeed taken to be the truth—also involves the careful manipulation of meaning and literalness. However, a statement to be taken for the truth must be carefully based in the listener's literal frame of reference. Lying is similar to acting, for acting is in one sense lying, and good acting, like successful lying, must be based on substantial realism. In fact, the quality and success of both lying and acting are primarily based on the realism they are able to interpret and project or portray.

Sorting the literal from the metaphorical, the logical from the analogical, the humorous from the serious, the lie from the truth, the real action from its playful representation, and correctly interpreting the multiple meanings and senses of these symbolic expressions is what thick description is all about as an ethnographic task. It is also what is absolutely necessary if we are to learn to converse successfully with other peoples, and thereby reduce the estrangement that divides us.

The sorting tasks of thick description require first and foremost a rather complete understanding of a people's literal frame of reference. Metaphor, humor, falsehood, and play are all based on and derived from literalness, and take on their unique character from the ways in which they modify and manipulate the literal frame of reference. Without some rather precise notions about the real and the literal, there would be nothing to manipulate, modify, falsify, or portray.

Navajo *k'é* terms signify a multitude of affective be

behavioral codes, and the extensive and complex ways in which Navajos use these terms can be baffling if one does not start with the correct literal frames of reference and then carefully work from there through various modifications, manipulations, and classifications. If we start with the assumption that *k'é* terms are kinship terms and that kinship terms ultimately or literally refer to kinsmen who are thought to share common substance, then we will be constantly trying to relate the data to an inappropriate and incorrect frame of reference, and any order we might find in the data will be inappropriately imposed on it instead of inherent in it.

The emphasis, focus, and literal frames of reference of Navajo concepts of *k'é* solidarity are found in affective action, not in static substance. This, of course, again demonstrates the Navajo interest in motion and action. *K'é* terms symbolize and classify various kinds of affective action. When kinship solidarity is symbolized in action rather than in substance, a whole new world of possible kinship relations unfolds. No longer does real or true kinship have to be restricted to those who share common substance; it can exist between any persons who act according to the behavior code of kinship.

In Navajo society everyone is addressed by a *k'é* term. This is in accord with the Navajo ideal of relating to everyone as a kinsman. Personal names are never used in address, and they are not used in reference when the person to whom the speaker is referring is in the presence of the speaker. Personal names isolate the individual and emphasize his distinctiveness and his separateness, failing to establish, express, or recognize any relationship between the speaker and the person addressed.

The Navajo emphasis on harmony and order as expressed by the term *hózhǫ́* is an emphasis on relatedness. It is impossible to have order and harmony among unrelated entities. *K'é* terms refer to forms of social harmony and order that are based in affective action. Rather than seeking to emphasize their independence, self-reliance, and separateness, and rather than seeking to escape bonds with others that involve continuous obligations of assistance and generosity, Navajos seek to relate themselves to others in their world, and seek to join in the vast system of interdependence that characterizes the social harmony and order of their world. Navajos find themselves and their fulfillment in life not in introspection, solitary meditation, or in assertions of their individuality or independence; they find their fulfillment in affective acts and bonds which unite and harmonize them with the social universe in which they live.

Navajos are vulnerable to the ill will of others. The will—the power of thought—can cause *hóchxǫ́* as well as *hózhǫ́*, and one can will misfortune and tragedy onto others through forms of witchcraft. Although careful, deliberate, and proper action can reduce the danger, and various ceremonies can create a substantial degree of immunity to the ill will of various Holy People, only the generosity, kindness, and cooperativeness expressed in affective action can reduce one's vulnerability to the ill will of other earth surface people. Through the affective actions found in forms of *k'é* solidarity a Navajo can transform potential ill will into good will. *K'é* refers to a system of good will, and through good will Navajos are able to create harmony and order and substantially reduce the existence of ill will in their world, and thereby their vulnerability to witchcraft.

With such an intensive emphasis on *k'é* solidarity and such an extensive use of *k'é* terms, it is not surprising that *k'é* terms have multiple meanings in both the scope of things to which they refer and in the degree of affective solidarity which they express. These terms are used both literally and metaphorically, seriously and humorously, carefully and casually, sincerely and pretentiously. If we are to understand the meanings and uses of these terms, we must first take great care in untangling and differentiating their multiple referents, and then we can begin to understand the meanings intended for each term in various contexts.

In describing and analyzing *k'é* terms, anthropologists have mistakenly assumed that the referents of these terms can be ascertained and identified by viewing them as labels for positions on the standard genealogical grid. Although there may be some value in such a genealogical representation of Navajo *k'é* terminology, an analysis of this type is inadequate, inappropriate, and misleading. Let us examine some of the reasons for this inadequacy and inappropriateness.

The genealogical grid in figure 5 shows the labels for both parents and their siblings.

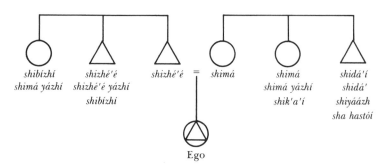

Fig. 5. Parental and Collateral Kin Terms

From this grid it can be seen that there are three labels for the position of father's brother and three labels for the position of mother's sister. If one asks a particular Navajo what the term for father's brother is, he may answer with any one of the three terms listed. He may or may not volunteer the other terms as alternate possibilities; nevertheless, upon further inquiry or suggestion, he will recognize the others as acceptable alternates. Some field workers have assumed that the first term volunteered by their informants is the one and only term their informants use for specified genealogical positions, and have thus developed essays on regional variation in Navajo kinship terminology (Freed and Freed, 1970). Others have found and illustrated that there are indeed alternate terms used for the same positions on the standard genealogical grid (Aberle, 1961:173–77; Landar, 1962:988–93; Shepardson and Hammond, 1970:227).

Why do the Navajos alternately call father's brothers *shizhé'é,* *shizhé'é yázhí,* or *shibízhí*? Thus far we have only three answers to this question. One answer is that it is due to regional variation (Freed and Freed, 1970:1442); a second answer is that it is a result of genuine fluctuation in Navajo linguistic forms and usages (Landar, 1962:995); a third answer is that it is due to genuine "fuzziness" and flexibility in Navajo kinship and social organization (Aberle, 1963:3). My response to this problem is that our inability to interpret correctly the reason for alternate and multiple terms for the same genealogical position is due to the fact that we are referring these terms to a standard genealogical grid that does not exist as such in the Navajo world. In other words, we are relating these terms to the wrong literal frame of reference, and we have not discovered the full range of referents that these terms have.

The term *shimá* has a very wide range of referents including, among others, one's mother by birth, the earth, the sheep herd, the corn field, and the mountain soil bundle. For us this reference to the earth as one's mother may seem to be a metaphorical use of the kinship idiom. To the Navajos, however, the earth is a living being, and it has an inner form who is Earth Woman, another one of the names of Changing Woman. Changing Woman is the being who gave life to the Navajos by creating the heads of the four original clans. It is she who sustains the life of her children today by producing food and other items of subsistence for them. Through rituals she bestows blessings on them and provides them with immunity from various dangerous things and protection from malevolent beings. It is she who was the first mother, the primordial life-giver and life-sustainer.

If one asks Navajos if the earth is like a mother rather than actually a mother, they will respond with surprise and wonder. In answering the question they will assert that the Earth as the outer form of Earth Woman or Changing Woman is not only an actual mother but that she is also the greatest of all mothers. In an excellent treatment of the "Symbolic Elements in Navajo Ritual," Louise Lamphere comes to the following conclusion:

> Navajo ritual identification and removal imply an alternative to Turner's analysis of Ndembu symbols, where concepts derived from bodily experiences are projected onto the natural and social world. . . . Rather than body processes being

relevant to classifying the world, concepts concerning the natural-supernatural world are relevant to interpreting body processes (1969:279).

If one assumes that there is a single, fixed, and context free primary meaning of *shimá*, then this frame of reference suggests that it is the human mother who resembles the Earth Mother, rather than vice versa. Mircea Eliade, looking at this matter from another perspective, came to a similar conclusion:

> This fundamental experience—that the human mother is only a representative of the telluric Great Mother—has given rise to countless customs. . . . The religious meaning of the custom is easy to see: generation and childbirth are microcosmic versions of a paradigmatic act performed by the earth; every human mother only imitates and repeats this primordial act of the appearance of life in the womb of the earth (1959:141–42).

In the Navajo frame of reference a mother is one who gives and sustains life (Witherspoon, 1975a:15–22), and by both of these definitions the earth is a mother to the earth surface people who are indeed her children.

The sheep herd and corn fields are also called mother. Werner and Begishe's informant put it this way:

(167) *dá'ák'eh wolyéii nimá át'é*
The one called farm is your mother.

. . . .

(129) *dibé wolyéii nimá át'é*
Those called sheep are your mother.

(130) *dibé iiná nilíinii át'é*
Sheep are life (1968:105,96).

These sentences seem to be literal in one sense and metaphorical in another sense. The corn fields and the sheep herd do in a very real and literal sense sustain the life of the Navajo, and in that sense they are indeed a mother to the Navajo. However, the sheep herd and the corn fields did not give life through birth to the Navajo, and in that sense they are not mothers to the Navajo. Most scholars would be willing to take this reference to the sheep herd as a mother to be strictly and totally a metaphor, but to refer to these sentences as metaphorical extensions of the idiom of kinship is an inadequate characterization of the meanings expressed in these sentences.

Navajos also refer to the sacred mountain soil bundle as *nihimá* 'our mother'. This use of the term *-má* expresses an association of the soil with Earth Woman, but its principal association with the concept of motherhood is found in the ways in which the mountain soil bundle sustains the lives of those who possess it through the protection from danger and evil that it provides them. The congruence between the relationship of the mountain soil bundle to its possessors or children and the relationship between Earth Mother and her children or even that between human mothers and their children is different from the congruence between the relationship of Earth Mother to her children and the relationship of the sheep herd or the corn field to their children.

Most words and linguistic expressions label concepts and conceptual classes, and these concepts and classes are all based on analogical propositions; that is, they lump together under one label things and events that are distinct and separate but which do in some ways resemble one another. No two oak trees—even two of the same variety in the same forest—ever resemble each other in exact detail, and even if their resemblance were exact, their position in space and their material constitution would be different. But because of their resemblance, we call them both oak trees. Earth Woman, human mothers, the sheep herd, corn fields, and the mountain soil bundle are all called *shimá*. It is not adequate or accurate, however, to say simply that some are mothers and some are not mothers but are metaphorical extensions of the concepts of motherhood. They are all mothers, but each one is a mother in a way that in part resembles the others but in part is distinct from the others.

If one drops the idea that there is a single primary meaning to the term *shimá* and rejects the notion that all other meanings are secondary or metaphorical, one can view, as Professor Raymond Kelly has suggested to me, all referents of the term *shimá* as informing each other, a case in which there is an exchange of meaning among all the referents. Professor Kelly cites the example of parishioners calling their parish priest "Father." This, he claims, is not merely an extension of the kin term to nonkin so as to inject the kinship pattern of amity into the priest-parishioner relationship. It also informs the meaning of "father" in the familial domain in such a way as to invest it with a priestly or sacred moral authority. Thus "father" is not a uniformly defined, distinctly bound category but a set of semantic elements that are analogically linked together.

By viewing all the referents of the term *shimá* as a set of semantic elements analogically linked together, we can see how they all inform the meaning of the term and participate in an exchange of meaning. All of the referents are mothers because they provide items of sustenance, but human mothers add a special touch of warmth and affection while the sacred mountain soil bundles provide protection from danger. The sheep herd provides security from starvation and poverty. The benevolence of Changing Woman provides immunity from various evil beings. The corn field emphasizes the fertility and fecundity of motherhood.

The Polysemy of *K'é* Terms

Navajo *k'é* terms have two frames of reference that are based on affective action. They refer to a set of relationships wherein giving birth provides the distinctive feature by which the relationship is defined. They also refer to a set of behavioral codes that can be defined as the generous giving of both emotional and physical sustenance. Moreover, *k'é* terms are not only polysemous with regard to these two frames of reference, they are also polysemous within the two frames of reference. Whereas the polysemy with regard to the giving of sustenance varies in scope and intensity, the polysemy with regard to giving birth varies in kind and type. The former type of polysemy is best thought of in terms of degrees or gradations on a continuum, while the latter form of polysemy, which refers to differences in type and kind, can best be understood in terms of a taxonomy.

The Navajo terms *k'é* and *k'éí* signify the difference between the two frames of reference discussed herein. *K'é* refers to behavioral codes based in affective action such as love, generosity, kindness, and so on. For the Navajo the expression of love, generosity, and kindness is particularly found in giving and sharing emotional and physical sustenance. It refers to various kinds of affective actions which vary in scope and intensity. When the ending *-í* is added to *k'é* it nominalizes *k'é*, the preverbal element, and turns it into a special kind of *k'é*. *K'éí* refers to the vast set of relationships that are initially defined by the features of giving birth and are further differentiated by the components of sex, generation, age, and lineality. This is also known as the clan or descent system of the Navajo.

A. *K'é* Terms and Descent Categories

The classes and categories of Navajo clan or *k'éí* relationships are amenable to distinctive feature analysis because they are at the most general level constructed and differentiated with regard to the absolute action of giving birth and the relatively definite and invariable attributes of sex, generation, lineality, and age. At the most general level these classes are strictly and solely defined by who gave the birth and for whom the birth was given. No clansman is more of a clansman than somebody else. On-going behavioral relationships or the lack of them have absolutely nothing to do with one's membership in any of these classes or categories.

The Navajo descent system includes six main categories: (1) mother's clan; (2) father's clan; (3) born for mother's clan; (4) born for father's clan; (5) clan for which mother is born; (6) clan for which father is born. A child becomes a member of his mother's clan, for it is that clan which give him birth. Although children are only given birth by their mother's clan, they are said to be born for their father's clan. The "born for" concept further relates a Navajo to those who are born for his clan and to those who are born for his father's clan. One is also related to the clans *for* which his mother and father are born. The feature of giving birth or "born of" establishes the ego's primary descent identity, while the "born for" concept establishes five additional categories of *k'éí* to which the ego is related.

Before going into a detailed analysis of the six categories outlined above, it is necessary to look at the broader social universe of which these descent categories are a part. *Diné,* the term for 'people', provides a linguistic boundary for the social universe of the Navajo. *Diné* are subdivided into two important kinds: (1) *Diyin Dine'é* (the supernaturals or Holy People); and (2) *nihokáá'dine'é* (the naturals or earth surface people). The earth surface people are further subdivided into the *Diné* (the Navajo) and the *ana'í* (aliens or non-Navajos). The *ana'í* are further subgrouped into various types of aliens, while the *Diné* are further subgrouped into approximately sixty matrilineally defined descent categories called *dine'é,* which refers to a particular kind of *Diné*. A taxonomical representation of these categories is provided in figure 6.

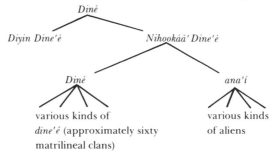

Fig. 6. Taxonomy of *Diné* (*Adapted from Witherspoon, 1975a:119*)

From this taxonomy it can be seen that the term *diné* has at least two levels or ranges of reference. Beyond these two levels, *diné* also refers to men as contrasted to women, and to young men as contrasted to older men.

Since the myth, apparently initiated by Redfield, that tribal

peoples believe they are "the people" is widely believed in anthropological circles, some may question that the most general
meaning of *diné* includes all people. The suffixing of an *-í* or *-é* on
a term makes it 'the particular one' or 'a special kind of'. Therefore, *nihokáá' dine'é* and *Diyin Dine'é* are special kinds of *diné*. If a
subcategory exists, there has to be a general category of which it is
a subcategory. If the most general referent of *diné* is 'the Navajos',
then *Diyin Dine'é* (Holy People) would have to be a kind of Navajo
which of course is ridiculous, and *nihookáá' dine'é* (earth surface
people) would not include non-Navajos which is obviously not the
case.

The term *diné* presents an interesting case of polysemy. In its
widest range of reference it means people; its second level of
meaning narrows this range to Navajo people; its third level of
meaning narrows the range to men as opposed to women; its
fourth level of meaning narrows the range to younger men as
opposed to older men. This form of polysemy where the range of
referents becomes narrower at each level of meaning is not uncommon, but it is very difficult for the anthropologist to sort out,
and it is very easy to see how the anthropologist and the informant each misconstrue what the other is asking and saying, especially when an interpreter is involved.

The discussion of the referents of *diné* is relevant to an analysis
of Navajo *k'é* terms for two reasons. First, *k'é* terms are concerned
with solidarity, and the higher referents of *diné* outline the social
universe in which *k'é* is the solidifier. Second, the semantic features and linguistic manipulations involved in an analysis of the
uses and referents of *diné* are directly applicable to or reappear in
the *k'é* terminology. The suffixing of an *-í* on *k'é* is the same kind
of grammatical operation as the suffixing of an *-é* on *diné*. *K'éí*
then becomes a particular kind of *k'é*. Let us now examine the
general classes and specific categories which constitute one's *k'éí*.

1. *Clan Which Gives Me Birth.* Navajos frequently say *táchii'nii*
(identifying their own clan) *éí shimá ádaat'é*, which translates 'all
those of my clan are *shimá*'. Thus the term *shimá* is used as a label

for all those in one's own clan. What this statement indicates is that the "person" or the "people" of my clan are *shimá* to me. In so labeling the person or people of his own clan, ego is not taking into consideration any attributes of the person or the people of his clan other than their descent identity. Within the descent or *k'éí* categories, the widest or most general range of meaning of *shimá* is *people of my own clan.*

If ego wishes to or thinks it appropriate to take into consideration the sex identity of those in his own clan, a male will consider all females of his clan to be *shimá,* and all males of his clan to be *shik'is.* A female will consider all the females of her clan to be *shimá,* while considering all the males of her clan to be *shiyáázh.* Thus a second level or more narrow range of reference of *shimá* is *females of my own clan.*

The next attribute of the person of his own clan that ego may wish to take into consideration is the generation of the person relative to ego's generation. A male considers all those females of his own clan who are two generations above him to be *shimá sání* (elderly or aged mother). Those females of his own clan who are one generation above ego are considered to be *shimá,* while those who are one generation below ego are considered to be *shimá yázhí.* Those two generations descending from ego are referred to as *sitsói.* Females of his own generation are considered *shilah.* The categories and labels are the same for a female except those one generation below her are referred to as *shich'é'é* instead of *shimá yázhí.* Here the referents of *shimá* have been further narrowed to *females of my clan who are one ascending generation from me.*

The next attribute of the person of his own clan which ego considers is that of lineal relative as opposed to collateral relative. A female who is one generation above ego and a lineal relative is considered *shimá,* while similar females who are not lineal relatives are considered *shimá yázhí.* At this point we have the most specific referent of *shimá*; it is *a female of my clan who is one generation above me and a lineal relative.* These ranges of meaning of *shimá* and the other categories and labels found in one's own clan are illustrated in the taxonomies of figure 7 (male ego) and figure 8 (female ego).

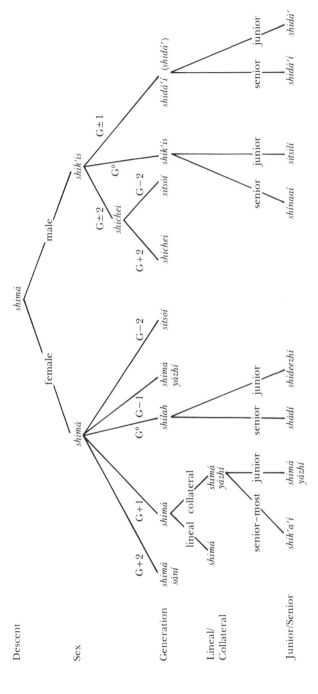

Fig. 7. Taxonomy of Mother's Clan (Male Ego) *(Adapted from Witherspoon, 1975a:122)*

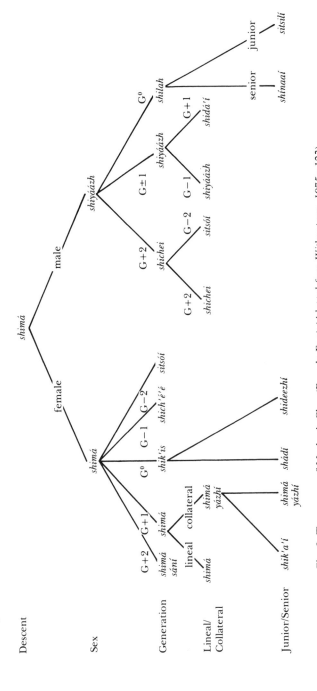

Fig. 8. Taxonomy of Mother's Clan (Female Ego) (*Adapted from Witherspoon, 1975a:123*)

2. *Clan for Which Ego Is Born.* A Navajo considers a person of the clan for which he is born to be *shizhé'é*. When considering the clan for which he is born as a collective entity, a Navajo refers to it as *shizhé'é*. In its widest range of reference, *shizhé'é* refers to *all those of the clan for which I am born.* When the attribute of lineal vs. collateral is considered, collateral relatives of the clan for which one is born are considered *shibízhí*, while the lineal relatives of this same clan are still considered *shizhé'é*. The attributes of lineal/collateral narrow the meaning of *shizhé'é* to *lineal relative of the clan for which I am born.*

When ego also considers the generation of the people of the clan for which he is born, collateral relatives of two ascending generations are considered to be *shinálí*. Those of one ascending generation or one or more descending generations are considered to be *shibízhí*. A female ego considers collateral relatives of her own generation to be *sizeedí*. A male ego leaves this node unlabeled and makes a mandatory sex distinction, calling males *shił naa'aash* and females *sizeedí*. Lineal relatives in this clan who are two ascending generations from ego are *shinálí*, while those one ascending generation from him are *shizhé'é*. Therefore, the most specific referent of *shizhé'é* is *lineal relative of one ascending generation of the clan for which I am born.* The taxonomy of this descent category is found in figure 9.

3. *Born for Own Clan.* A male considers all those born for his clan to be *sha'áłchíní*. A female considers all those born for her clan to be *sizeedí*. A male next subdivides this descent category on the basis of sex, considering males to be *shiye'* and females to be *sitsi'*. A female makes no distinctions in this category based on sex. When generation is considered, a female considers those plus or minus two generations to be *shinálí*, those plus or minus one generation to be *shibízhí*, and those of her own generation to be *sizeedí*. A male considers males of his own generation to be *shił naa'aash*, males one descending generation to be *shiye'* and males two descending generations to be *shinálí*. He considers females of his own generation to be *sizeedí*, females one descending generation

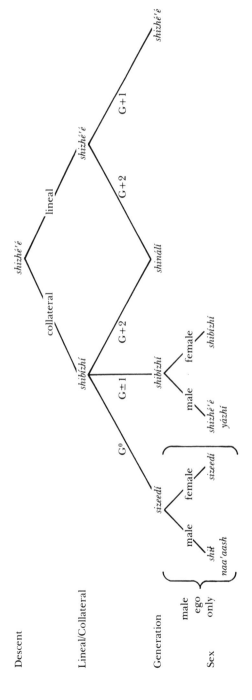

Fig. 9. Taxonomy of Father's Clan (*Adapted from Witherspoon, 1975a:123*)

to be *sitsi'*, and females two descending generations to be *shináli*. The taxonomies of this descent category are illustrated in figure 10.

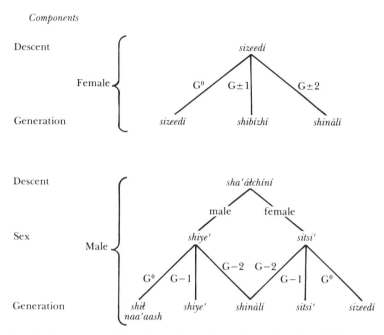

Fig. 10. Taxonomy of Those Born for Mother's Clan (*Adapted from Witherspoon, 1975a:124*)

4. *Born for Same Clan.* Those who are born for the same clan consider themselves to be either *shik'is* or *shilah* to each other. There is no cover term for this category. In this category there is a mandatory sex discrimination according to which those of the same sex call each other *shik'is* and those of the opposite sex call each other *shilah*. When sibling order or relative age is considered, older females are called *shádí* while older males are called *shínaaí*. Younger females are called *shideezhí* while younger males are called *sitsilí*. The taxonomies of this descent category are found in figure 11.

5. *Clan for Which Shimá Is Born.* A person of this descent category is considered to be *shichei*. When the attribute of sex is con-

sidered, males are still considered to be *shichei* while females of this category are called *shimá sání*.

6. *Clan for Which Shizhé'é Is Born.* All persons—male and female, old and young, lineal and collateral—in this category are considered to be *shinálí*.

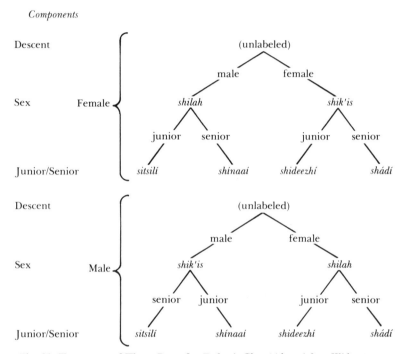

Fig. 11. Taxonomy of Those Born for Father's Clan (*Adapted from Witherspoon, 1975a:124*)

B. *K'é* Terms and Behavioral Relationships

The *k'é* terms which label the discrete and invariable classes and categories of *k'éí* also refer to a set of culturally defined behavioral relationships. The focal point or dominant standard of this set of behavioral relationships is found in the solidary behavior that characterizes the mother-child bond. This central bond is modified by the culturally significant concepts of sex, generation, sibling order, and distance. Elsewhere I have provided a full description of how these concepts modify the basic code of *k'é* solidarity (1975a:49–55). The code of *k'é* can be generalized as including kindness, helpfulness, cooperativeness, peacefulness, and so on, and can be specified as involving the giving and sharing of physical and emotional sustenance. Among various kinsmen this code varies more in intensity than it does in kind.

Intensity is something that varies in degrees and can appropriately be conceived of in terms of a continuum rather than in terms of discretely defined classes. The concept of distance forms a continuum that varies in degrees or amounts and is, therefore, an appropriate dimension on which intensity can be labeled and defined.

Distance of relationship is conceived of both in terms of socio-geographic and genealogical space. Socio-geographic distance is reflected in terms of members of the same household group as opposed to members of separate households. Members of the same household live in closer proximity to each other, share common interests and property, and are expected to be more intensely related to each other than to those of separate households. This correlation further extends to members of the same residence group, outfit, and community (called a chapter). There is in Navajo society a corresponding degree of geographic distance interwoven with the social distance created by membership in and residence with distinct social units. For example, where several households in the same residence group are headed by individuals who are siblings, the households headed by sisters tend to be clustered together while the household of a brother is marked by greater distance from the core cluster of households.

Navajo concepts of genealogy or genealogical space do not follow the standard paradigm which is ubiquitous in anthropology. In Navajo culture there are only two primary or unmediated relationships. These exist between husband and wife and between mother and child. The mother is the focal point in both of these relationships, for both involve a different relationship to her womb. It is she who provides the link between the father and the children born for (not of or by) him. Genealogical distance is basically calculated by the number of linking bonds that exist between the individual and his relatives. Because the mother-child bond is much more intense and secure than the husband-wife bond, relationships linked together by, for instance, three links wherein one of the links is a husband-wife bond have to be considered to be more distant (thus less intense) than relationships linked together by three maternal bonds.

Concepts of sex, generation, and relative age also express intensity through distance. The relationship of two relatives who are three links apart but of opposite sexes is more distant and thus less intense than the relationship of two relatives who are also three links apart but who are of the same sex. Other things being equal, relatives separated by a generational difference of one or two generations are not as close as those of the same generation. Relative age within the same generation often determines the senior/junior aspect of a relationship but this is more of a modification of kind or type than it is of distance or intensity.

Figures 12 and 13 illustrate how genealogical distance is structured according to Navajo concepts and definitions. The keen observer will note that the *k'é* terms listed on these figures are the same as those which labeled classes and categories of *k'éí*. Herein we see the polysemy of these terms. They both label classes of relatives and they label the intensity of relationships. Labeling the world of kinship and kin categories is very different from labeling other kinds of reality such as objects at rest (which will be discussed in detail in the next section of this chapter). In labeling and classifying objects at rest, ego creates class and order based on the attributes and characteristics of the objects, not on his relationship to the objects or classes. With regard to kinship, however, ego's relationship to the category or class is extremely important, and *k'é* terms label and classify kinds and degrees of relationship as well as classes of relatives. Labeling the category as well as ego's relationship to the category seems to be part and parcel of the same thing, and that appears to be the reason for using the same set of terms for both jobs. This polysemy of *k'é* terms is not usu-

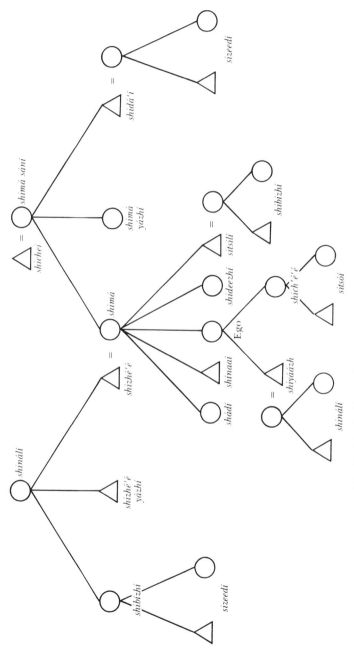

Fig. 12. Navajo Categories of Genealogical Distance (Female Ego)

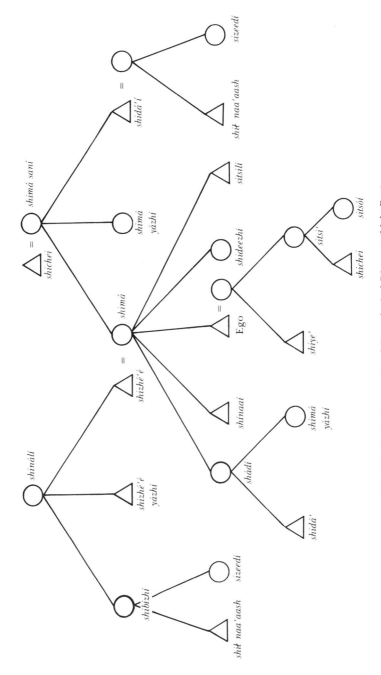

Fig. 13. Navajo Categories of Genealogical Distance (Male Ego)

ally distinguished as such by anthropologists and linguists, but it is distinguished by the Navajo, as I will show later in the discussion of the usage of $k'\acute{e}$ terms.

The relationship of ego to various categories of relatives may be ordered in terms of intensity. Such an ordering of these categories would naturally be based on the dimension of distance including, in order of priority, genealogical, sexual, and generational distance. This order of priority was arrived at intuitively, based on my exposure to and knowledge of Navajo culture. The charts in tables 1 and 2 illustrate how the eighteen relationships shown in figures 12 and 13 are ordered on the dimension of intensity, with relationship one as the most intense and relationship eighteen as the least intense of the set.

TABLE 1

Female Ego

		Distance		
	Relationship	Genealogical	Sex	Generation
1.	*shimá* (Mo)	1M	1	1
2.	*shich'é'é* (Da)	1M	1	1
3.	*shiyáázh* (Son)	1M	2	1
4.	*shádí* (OZ)	2M	1	0
5.	*shideezhí* (YZ)	2M	1	0
6.	*shimá sání* (MGM)	2M	1	2
7.	*sitsói* (MGCh)	2M	1 or 2	2
8.	*shínaaí* (OB)	2M	2	0
9.	*sitsilí* (YB)	2M	2	0
10.	*shizhé'é* (Fa)	1M + 1C	2	1
11.	*shimá yázhí* (MoZ)	3M	1	1
12.	*shidá'í* (MoBr)	3M	2	1
13.	*shinálí* (PGM)	2M + 1C	1 or 2	2
14.	*shichei* (PGFa)	2M + 1C	2	2
15.	*shibízhí* (FaZ)	3M + 1C	1 or 2	1
16.	*shizhé'é yázhí* (FaBr)	3M + 1C	2	1
17.	*shizeedí* (CC)	4M + 1C	1 or 2	0

Note: M = maternal bond; C = conjugal or husband-wife bond; Sex 1 = same sex; Sex 2 = opposite sex; Generation 0 = same generation; Generation 1 = one generation removed from ego; Generation 2 = two generations removed from ego.

TABLE 2

Male Ego

		Distance		
	Relationship	Genealogical	Sex	Generation
1.	shimá (Mo)	1M	2	1
2.	shínaaí (OBr)	2M	1	0
3.	sitsilí (YBr)	2M	1	0
4.	shádí (OZ)	2M	2	0
5.	shideezhí (YZ)	2M	2	0
6.	shimá sání (MGM)	2M	2	2
7.	shizhé'é (Fa)	1M + 1C	1	1
8.	shiye' (So)	1M + 1C	1	1
9.	sitsi' (Da)	1M + 1C	2	1
10.	shidá'í (MoBr)	3M	1	1
11.	shimá yázhí (MoZ)	3M	2	1
12.	shichei (MGF)	2M + 1C	1	2
13.	sitsói (MGCh)	2M + 1C	1 or 2	2
14.	shinálí (PGF)	2M + 1C	2	2
15.	shizhé'é yázhí (FaBr)	3M + 1C	1	1
16.	shibízhí (FaZ)	3M + 1C	1 or 2	1
17.	shił naa'aash (CC)	4M + 1C	1	0
18.	sizeedí (CC)	4M + 1C	2	0

Note: M = maternal bond; C = conjugal or husband-wife bond; Sex 1 = same sex; Sex 2 = opposite sex; Generation 0 = same generation; Generation 1 = one generation removed from ego; Generation 2 = two generations removed from ego.

These tables only deal with distance within the genealogical framework of the Navajo. In actual usage, the factor of socio-geographical distance is also important and is taken into consideration in defining the relationship deemed appropriate for two particular individuals. *K'é* term usage, particularly with regard to everyday patterns of address, is a matter of context, but the cultural constants which, to a large extent, define the social context are concepts of genealogical and socio-geographical distance.

C. *K'é* Term Usage

Although both sets of referents (categories and relationships) of *k'é* terms are based in forms of affective action (giving birth and giving sustenance), these two sets appear to be structured according to the fundamental dualism of all phenomena—static and active. The classes and categories of *k'éí* which were outlined earlier are static and invariable, while the relationships labeled by *k'é* terms vary in intensity and are altered by social context and idiosyncratic preferences and needs.

The six classes of *k'éí* are not concerned with intensity and are not differentiated in terms of distance. Everyone in ego's clan is a *shimá* to ego. With regard to descent identity, there is no one in ego's clan who is more of a clansman or a *shimá* than anyone else. Ego's place in two of these classes and his relationship to the other four of these classes is fixed by his birth. The clan into which ego is born establishes the kind of *Diné* he is, and this identity is static, invariable, and unalterable. The "born for" concept relates ego to four more classes of *Diné* and places him in the class born for his father's clan. These additional classes are also clearly and unalterably defined and their static boundaries are precisely drawn. The attributes by which members of these classes are further distinguished and the classes subdivided are also static in nature. One's sex identity or generation with regard to ego are basically unalterable, and a lineal relative can never become a nonlineal relative.

The behavioral relationships to which *k'é* terms refer vary in intensity and change according to situation and context. The use of these terms and the meanings they convey correspond to the flow of social action and environmental change. In this area the relationship between two particular kinsmen is not fixed and changes with time and context, for most relationships are constantly being defined and redefined. As these relationships are changed and altered, they may be said to move and to flow, demonstrating their basically active nature.

The static and active dimensions of the polysemy of *k'é* terms basically follow in usage the analytical distinction of terms of reference and terms of address. The static categories are basically terms of reference, for they primarily serve to allow ego to classify and order his social universe neatly. The invariable and unalterable nature of these classes and categories gives ego a secure framework within which to place himself. The active dimension of the meanings of *k'é* terms allows ego to constantly define and redefine his relationships according to the ebb and flow of social life. These active meanings are primarily reflected in terms of address.

Although accurate and complete data on the usage of *k'é* terms cannot be obtained from interviewing informants, there are two questions that an informant may be asked that distinguish between the terms that label static classes and the terms that label active relationships. When seeking the former kind of information or, generally speaking, terms of reference, one should ask, *Hait'áo nik'éí át'é?* This question asks 'How is he or she *k'éí* to you?' or 'How according to classes of *k'éí* are you related to him or her?' When seeking information on how an informant addresses a particular relative one should ask *Hait'áo k'é bidíní?* This question asks, 'How, according to *k'é*, do you address him or her?' It is common for these questions to be answered by different terms.

Although there are some occasions when a Navajo uses in address a term which labels *k'éí* categories and there are times when terms expressing relationships of *k'é* are used in reference, it is usually not very difficult to differentiate one use and meaning from the other. A Navajo uses *k'é* terms in everyday interaction with people whom he knows well. In this context his particular and current relationships with other kinsmen are of utmost importance, and it is the intensity and to some extent the type of relationship which are designated by *k'é* terms of address. As ego's relationship with a particular kinsman changes, he selects a different term with which to address his kinsman. Thus *k'é* terms of address stay in touch with the everyday flow of social life.

When a man and his wife and children reside at his mother's home, the children of the man usually call their paternal grandmother *shimá sání* which is normally used for only the maternal grandmother. Such children also call their father's sister's children by sibling terms instead of those commonly used for cross-cousins. These children also call their father's sisters *shimá yázhí*, a term appropriately used for mother's sisters. If asked why they do this, Navajos will say they do it out of politeness or that these terms better express the way they feel about their relationships with these particular relatives. These examples illustrate how socio-geographic distance alters the intensity of kinship relations, and these alterations are expressed in everyday *k'é* term usage.

Idiosyncratic feelings, needs, and preferences are also important factors that influence the particular kind and intensity of any given relationship. Cross-cousins who become particularly fond of each other call each other by sibling terms, regardless of residence. A woman who takes a special interest in or gives special care to a brother's son will be called *shimá*, not *shibízhí*. A maternal grandmother who rears her daughter's child will be called *shimá* instead of *shimá sání*. The same would be true for any woman who rears a child.

Although Navajos have a great deal of freedom and flexibility in ordering and describing the particular relationships they have with people with whom they interact on a daily or regular basis, there are two constraints on this flexibility. One is that sex identity is never altered. Ego can never address a man with a term appropriate only for a female relative, and a female relative may never be addressed by a term such as *shizhé'é* (father) or *shínaaí* (brother). The second restraint is that the degree of intensity expressed by *k'é* terms may, in a sense, only be increased—not decreased. It is acceptable to address a *shimá sání* (maternal grandmother) by the term *shimá* (mother), but it is never polite or appropriate to call a mother by the term appropriate for a maternal grandmother or other more distant relative. Where a genetrix has neglected or deserted her child, the child will never address her with any term other than *shimá*. The child may refuse to call her *shimá* and may say *Éí doo shineesą́ą da, áko doo shimá át'ée da* 'She did not rear me or give me sustenance; therefore, she is not my mother', but the child cannot turn the genetrix into a paternal grandmother or any other more distant relative.

A better example of these patterns of usage occurs when a boy happens to be raised in the home of his mother's brother. In such a case, the boy will call his mother's brother's wife *shimá* (mother) but he will not call his mother's brother *shizhé'é* (father), because a father is considered to be a more distant relative than a mother's brother (see tables 1 and 2). There is a standardized ideal of intensity for ego's relationship to every category on the Navajo genealogical chart. Where the actual intensity of a relationship is greater than the standard, terms expressing this greater intensity may be used; but the reverse of this is impolite and unacceptable.

Language not only classifies experience, it also controls it; it not only defines situations, it also determines them. *K'é* terms do not just represent social reality, they order it. To address a person by a particular *k'é* term does more than just describe the relationship; it orders the relationship toward a particular goal, a standardized ideal. Unlabeled and undefined relationships are ambiguous and variable. The *k'é* term clarifies the ambiguity and codifies the movement and variance of social relationships.

K'é terms order social relationships by directing and relating them to an ideal code. Accordingly it is unacceptable to use *k'é* terms to order relationships toward an ideal of intensity that is less than the norm for a particular set of kinsmen. The Navajo thinking seems to be that it is never acceptable to lower the ideal but that it is acceptable to increase or enhance it. Here again we see how the Navajos use the power of language to control reality and direct it to desirable ends. It is also not accidental that this occurs with regard to the essentially active *k'é* terms, the terms of address (i.e., speech).

Terms which assign people to various discrete classes of *k'éí* are primarily used for classifying strangers. When strangers meet they inquire into each other's descent identities, and from these they determine how to categorize each other. The first question asked is *Há'át'íish dine'é nílí?* 'What kind of a *Diné* are you?' or *Háísh danimá* 'Who are your mothers?' One usually responds by saying something like "I am a Bitterwater *Diné*," or "Bitterwater *Diné* are my mothers." The next question then is *Háísh danizhé'é?* 'Who are your fathers?' The questions may then proceed to the clans for which one's mother and father are born.

If one man discovers that another man is of his same clan, he may say, *Bitterwater* (identifying the clan) *éí shimá ádaat'é. Yá'át'ééh shik'is*. This translates 'Bitterwater people are my mothers. Hello, my brother.' What this man is saying is that a person of the Bitterwater clan, without distinguishing or differentiating characteristics, is a *shimá* to him, but actually when he proceeds to address the person, he selects a term which acknowledges the masculinity of the person addressed.

When strangers meet, their sex identities are usually obvious. Therefore, in addressing each other, strangers always use terms that are appropriate for the sex of the person addressed. The descent identities of the stranger are not, however, obvious, nor is the age of the stranger unmistakable. Where such important attributes of the stranger are not known, one is expected to assume the closest possible relationship. This means that when descent identities are not known, the terms used will always be those used for close relationships within one's own clan. When the descent identities and other relevant attributes are known, then the more specific, narrow-ranged terminology found at the lower levels of the taxonomies presented earlier is utilized in designating the relationship of any two kinsmen.

If two people discover that according to descent identities they are not related (which is the exception, not the rule), they continue to refer to and to address each other as kinsmen, normally using terms appropriate for members of the same clan. If they did not do this, people would say they were unfriendly, impolite, and not thinking according to *k'é*. The rule is that whenever in doubt or whenever there is no specific connection, the polite thing to do is to address the other person by a term which suggests the closest possible relationship.

The discrete and invariable categories of *k'éí* primarily function to order and classify the strange and the unknown, and to establish ties and bonds between ego and people of the wider social universe of which ego is a part, but with which he has only sporadic and distant contact. Accordingly, those related according to *k'éí* are expected to provide a place to sleep and eat for each other when one is traveling in a strange area. The *k'éí* categories also provide a person with an extensive network of relatives upon whom he may call for assistance when he needs to amass a large amount of food and wealth in order to put on a major ceremony. Furthermore, these categories divide up the wider social universe into two important categories: marriageable and unmarriageable. One is not supposed to marry anyone who is related to him or her according to any of these categories. The behavioral code associated with relationships of *k'éí* can be summarized as follows: (1) hospitality; (2) ceremonial cooperation; and (3) exogamy.

Because people are often related to each other in more than one way and because *k'é* terms refer both to behavioral relationships and to discrete categories of relatives, it is not uncommon for people to address each other by different terms in different contexts or even by two terms in the same context. This is a common practice in both myths and rituals, and is illustrated in the following prayer taken from Blessingway:

> From the beginning I fully know of it.
> Long ago one [he] was thinking of it.
> Long ago one [he] spoke of it.
> I am indeed its child.
> Absolutely I am Earth's child.
> I am indeed its grandchild.
> (Wyman, 1970:152)

D. Conclusion: Relationship and Category

Kinship terms are somewhat unusual in that they are both labels for categories and labels for the relationships between categories. With regard to figure 14, a legitimate question can be raised as to whether the term *shimá* is a label for the category 'mother' or is a label for the relationship between the categories of ego and his mother. The basis of this question is whether the term refers primarily to the category and is extended by association to the relationship between the categories, or whether it refers primarily to the relationship (behavioral code) between the categories and by extension to the category with which ego is so related.

Fig. 14. Relationship of Mother and Child

In the Navajo case I think it is clear that the term *shimá* and other *k'é* terms have two frames of reference, and therefore the concept of polysemy is more appropriate for the analysis of *k'é* terms than the distinction between literal and metaphorical meanings. Where *k'é* terms are used to label the categories of *k'éí*, they primarily refer to the discrete categories and not to ego's relationship to each of the categories of each class. Associated with these categories is a behavioral code that I summarized as (1) hospitality, (2) ceremonial cooperation, and (3) exogamy. This behavioral code is not the basis for the use of these terms or for the definition of the categories. If a woman is a member of ego's clan, she is a *shimá* to ego regardless of how they behave toward each other. If he ignores the behavioral code associated with the category of *shimá* and marries her, she remains a *shimá* to him.

In the polysemy of *k'é* terms there is another frame of reference wherein *k'é* terms refer primarily to the behavioral codes by which ego and his kinsmen are related, rather than to the categories of kinsmen associated with these behavioral codes. The behavioral code which takes priority in this case can be generalized as intense, diffuse, and enduring solidarity, expressed particularly in acts of kindness and in the giving and sharing of sustenance. This code constitutes the basis of all kinship relations, modified only by the concepts of distance, generation, sex, and relative age. The kin categories illustrated in figures 12 and 13 are the categories associated with this behavioral code and its modifications. The fact that these terms primarily refer to the relationships between ego and his kinsmen is continually manifested when ego addresses his kinsmen by terms that express and reflect his relationship to them in behavioral terms rather than in actual genealogical terms.

Ideally in both cases—the *k'éí* categories and the *k'é* relationships—the term used should express both the categorical position of the relative and ego's actual behavioral relationship to the relative. When there is a divergence from the ideal, ego gives preference to the categorical position or place of the relative when his frame of reference is the *k'éí* categories, but he gives preference to his actual behavioral relationship when his frame of reference is the behavioral code of *k'é*. Figure 15 illustrates these distinctions.

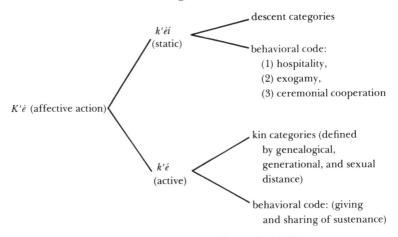

Fig. 15. Static and Active Categories of *K'é*

Figure 15 shows that *k'éí* is the marked term with regard to *k'é*. As was noted earlier, *k'éí* is a special kind of *k'é*. It does not seem to me to be simply coincidental that *k'éí*, the marked class, expresses the static dimension of *k'é*. In the Navajo view of the world, the static is always defined with regard to the active, the static being defined as the temporary withdrawal of motion. This seems to express the idea that the static dimension of nonmotion is a kind of motion, rather than motion being a kind of nonmotion. The focal point of this defining feature is motion or activity, and thus inactivity or nonmotion is linguistically marked as a special kind of activity or motion.

As elsewhere in Navajo culture the emphasis here is on the active relationships of *k'é*. The static categories which are relatively insignificant in Navajo social life are primarily used to classify strangers and to find hospitable homes in distant places. The *k'é* relationships express and reflect the on-going everyday patterns of Navajo social life. These relationships form the basis of both domestic and local community organization and solidarity. It is on these relationships that a Navajo primarily depends for his life and sustenance.

The emphasis given to relationships of *k'é* is also shown in the practice of calling everyone, regardless of descent identity or genealogical relationship, by a *k'é* term. This is practiced not only with regard to unrelated strangers and even non-Navajos, but also with regard to affines. Affines do not normally address each other with affinal terms, for this is considered to be impolite. Affinal terms express the categories into which affines can be placed, but they do not express intense and solidary behavioral relationships. Because the Navajo golden rule is to treat everyone as a kinsman, affines, strangers, nonclansmen, and even aliens are addressed by *k'é* terms. These terms not only categorize the social universe, but relate ego to everyone in that universe. They are even applied literally to nonhumans, for when one relies on the sheep herd for his life and sustenance, the sheep herd is his mother.

The Navajo have taken the dualistic dimensions of the *k'é* bond, giving birth and giving sustenance, and organized them according to the basic metaphysical propositions of static and active. From these they have developed, respectively, a descent system which orders and arranges the social universe into static categories, and a social system which organizes social life into flowing and active patterns. The former seems primarily to meet an intellectual need for order and arrangement, while the latter meets a physical need for sustenance and an emotional need for attachment. The former is probably related to Navajo aesthetics (in the sense of imposing order and arrangement on the universe), while the latter is inextricably related to, if not the foundation of, Navajo ethics. An understanding of these two dimensions of $k'\acute{e}$ solidarity will take us a long way toward bridging the estrangement we feel, for these constitute the ways according to which Navajos bridge the estrangement they might feel between themselves and the social universe in which they live.

III. CLASSIFYING OBJECTS AT REST

When a speaker of Navajo describes an object at rest, he places the object in one of 225 categories. All objects at rest fall into one of fifteen general categories based on observable qualities of animateness, size, position, cohesiveness, rigidity, shape, and degree of containment. Each of these fifteen general categories are subdivided into fifteen basic categories which are differentiated by the variables of plurality, grouping, and patterning, making a total of 225 categories of objects at rest.

The fifteen general categories are signified by the verb stem. The neuter prefix si indicates that the state of the object is static and durative, while the stem ($t\acute{q}$ in $sit\acute{q}$) designates the general category to which the object is assigned. The absence of a person marker indicates third person. Thus a pencil at rest is referred to by the term $sit\acute{q}$ because of its long, cylindrical shape, but a book is referred to by the term $si'\acute{q}$ because of its box-like shape. A sheet of paper is referred to by the term $si\!\#tsooz$ because of its thinness and its flexibility. A rope, like a pencil, is long and cylindrical but it is referred to by the term $sil\acute{a}$ because of its flexibility.

The various verb stems listed above do not label a class of objects, as Hoijer (1945) and nearly everyone else have apparently assumed, but label conceptual categories into which various ob-

---

Section III represents an enlarged and adapted version of "Navajo Categories of Objects at Rest," by Gary Witherspoon, published in *American Anthropologist* 73:110–27.

jects may be perceived to fit according to their position and attributes. Thus a blanket spread out is referred to by the term *sikaad* while the same blanket when folded is referred to by the term *siłtsooz*. If the blanket is piled (unfolded) in a corner somewhere it may be referred to as *siyį́*. Water in a bucket is *siká̧*, but water in a lake is *siyį́*. Wool in a pile is referred to by the term *sijool*, but wool in a sack is *siyį́*. A dog in a sitting position is referred to by the term *sidá*, but a dog in a standing position is *sizį́*, while a dog lying down is referred to by the term *sitį́*.

The conceptual categories discussed herein are very difficult to define, and no one has been able to provide anything but a very crude definition or a very rough gloss of what components distinguish one category from another. Hoijer says that *si'á̧* refers to a round object (1945:18), but that does not explain why boxes, books, houses, blocks, bricks, rocks, and knives are also put in this category. Hoijer (1945:19) says that *sitá̧* refers to a long object but that does not explain why a square picture or a rectangular but thin board are also put in the *sitá̧* class. *Sizį́* is said to refer to a living being but that does not explain why it also refers to iconic representations of animate beings and to such things as cars, trucks, and airplanes.

A very great variety of objects can be placed in one or more of these fifteen general categories, and it is no easy task to figure out exactly what characterizes or defines each of the categories, and on exactly what dimensions the categories are differentiated from each other. After hearing these terms used for fifteen years and using and misusing them myself for fifteen years, I am finally ready to try to define these categories in more precise terms than they have heretofore been defined, although I do not assume that these definitions will be the last or the definitive analysis of these categories. In analyzing these categories, I will provide a componential definition of each of the categories illustrating how each term is different from the others according to one or more components.

It seems to me that these cultural categories developed from sets of binary distinctions made on the basis of the inherent potential to move or be moved that various objects at rest were deemed to possess. Thus the initial binary distinction is between animate and inanimate objects. Animate beings are further divided into erect and nonerect categories. Beings capable of standing erect such as horses, dogs, and people are deemed to have greater capacity for movement than those which only lie and crawl such as snakes and turtles. Similarly, a person or animal in a standing or fully erect position is better ready to move than a person or animal in a sitting or semierect position. To extend this proposition even further, Navajos use the preverbal particle *dah* with *sidá* to indicate that a person is sitting on a chair or something similar as opposed to someone sitting on the ground or floor—a much more difficult position from which to move.

As is shown in figure 16, the inanimate category is first divided into the binary categories of contained and noncontained. Things in the contained categories are obviously less able or ready to move or be moved than those in the noncontained categories. In the contained category, that contained by a rigid container such as a barrel is less able to move than that contained in a nonrigid container such as a paper or cloth sack.

Noncontained categories are next divided into cohesive and incohesive classes. The greater the cohesiveness of an object the greater is its ability to stay at rest. The greater incohesive within the incohesive category (*sijool*) refers to such things as a pile or bunch of feathers, hair, or wool. Such incohesive entities can easily be moved by wind. The lesser incohesive within the incohesive category includes such items as mud and other mushy substances. These substances are constantly moving—changing forms, being formed and reformed, or transformed. Cohesive entities and substances are much less susceptible to being moved or transformed.

Cohesive entities are further divided into the binary classes of proportional and nonproportional. Proportional is used here to refer to an object that is relatively equal in its three dimensions. Nonproportional is used here to refer to an object which is excessively out of proportion along one of its dimensions; that is, it is very long, very narrow, or very thin. Essentially a proportional

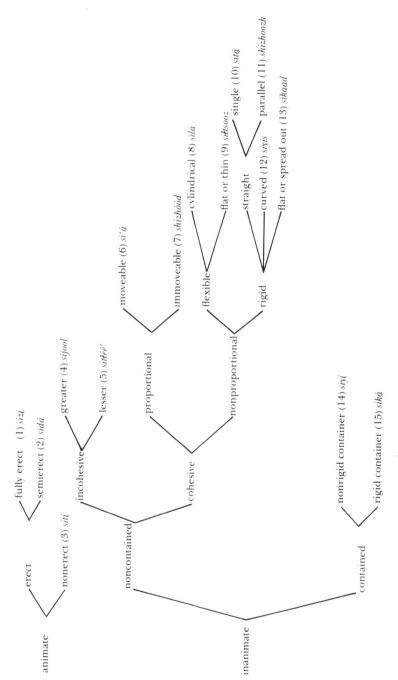

Fig. 16. Structure of Navajo Classificatory Verbs

123

item is more erect than a nonproportional item which tends to hug the ground or floor. The more erect, more proportional object can be more easily rolled and is less wind resistant. The categories *si'á* and *shizhóód* are distinguished by the factor of moveability. Things classed as *shizhóód* are much larger and heavier than those classed as *si'á*.

The nonproportional or nonerect classes are next divided into rigid and flexible classes. Items which fit into the flexible categories obviously are more subject to movement, alteration, or transformation than items that fit into the rigid category. The flexible category is further subdivided into a category for somewhat round or cylindrical objects such as ropes or body organs such as the heart, liver, lungs, or stomach and a category for flat or thin objects such as paper or cloth. The round or cylindrical objects are clearly more able to be moved by rolling than items that lie flat against some surface. Rigid items are divided into classes of flat, curved, or straight objects. It is easier to roll a long, straight item (*sitá*) such as a pencil than it is to roll a curved item (*siyis*) such as a bow or a spread out bunch of trees or a clump of bushes (*sikaad*).

By following the definitions provided above and illustrated in figure 16, it is possible to provide componential definitions of each of the fifteen terms (table 3).

The linear ordering of the fifteen terms is an attempt to arrange them in a sequence from the most moveable (number one) to the least moveable (number fifteen). As with the definitions themselves, this ordering is not assumed to be necessarily definitive. It is just an attempt to identify and scale the rationale behind these conceptual categories and the structural patterns inherent in them. Figure 16 also illustrates how each of the categories may have evolved in a historical or developmental sense.

It is of special interest here that such things as cars, trucks, and airplanes are put in the animate category of erect beings (*sizí*). In the classifications discussed in section I of this chapter, cars, trucks, and airplanes are not, however, considered to be animate beings. The difference seems to be that in terms of the classifications based on who can act upon whom, intelligence and will

TABLE 3

	1	2	3	4	5	6	7
				Number of Components by Which Each Term Is Defined			
1. *sizí*	animate	fully erect					
2. *sidá*	animate	semierect					
3. *sitį́*	animate	nonerect					
4. *sijool*	inanimate	noncontained	incohesive	greater			
5. *sitłéé'*	inanimate	noncontained	incohesive	lesser			
6. *si'ą́*	inanimate	noncontained	cohesive	proportional	moveable		
7. *shizhóód*	inanimate	noncontained	cohesive	proportional	immoveable		
8. *silá*	inanimate	noncontained	cohesive	nonproportional	flexible	cylindrical	
9. *sitłsooz*	inanimate	noncontained	cohesive	nonproportional	flexible	flat or thin	
10. *sitą́*	inanimate	noncontained	cohesive	nonproportional	rigid	straight	singular
11. *shizhoozh*	inanimate	noncontained	cohesive	nonproportional	rigid	straight	parallel
12. *síyís*	inanimate	noncontained	cohesive	nonproportional	rigid	curved	
13. *síkaad*	inanimate	noncontained	cohesive	nonproportional	rigid	flat or spread out	
14. *síyį́*	inanimate	contained	nonrigid container				
15. *síką́*	inanimate	contained	rigid container				

or intent are also essential to the definition of animate. If one says *Chidí hastiin yik'iilwod* 'The car ran over the man', the structure of the sentence makes it appear that the car attacked the man with will, intent, or premeditation. Such a sentence is unacceptable and absurd in the Navajo world because cars do not think and are not self-directing. In fact, in terms of its capacity to will and perform actions upon other beings, a car cannot even run over a ground squirrel or an ant. A car is classed as an inanimate object because it has no mind and is not capable of thought, intent, or speech.

Whereas classifications concerned with who can act upon whom are based on internal, inherent capacities for self-directed animation, the classificatory verb stems concerned with objects at rest are based on external, observable performances of movement or animation. In the latter case there appears to be no particular interest in cause and effect, subject and object, or actor and acted upon. The former set of classifications seems to be more concerned with underlying metaphysical assumptions and ultimate causal relationships, whereas the latter is simply concerned with the apparent and observable characteristics and characteristic behavior of the various entities. These two different classifications of the world seem to follow the Navajo pattern of dividing up the world into inner and outer forms. The former set of classifications appears to be really classifications of inner forms, which initiate and control thought, speech, and action. The latter set of classifications seems to be exclusively concerned with the visible attributes and characteristic behavior of outer forms.

Once a speaker of Navajo has placed an entity or entities in one of the fifteen general classes, he must next place the entity or entities into one of fifteen basic categories that are based on and differentiated by the variables of plurality, grouping, and patterning. The paradigm illustrated in figure 17 shows how the fifteen basic categories within each of the fifteen general categories are concatenated. The variables of plurality, grouping, and patterning will be discussed in detail below, followed by a general discussion of how these intersect to provide componential definitions of each of the fifteen basic categories illustrated in figure 17.

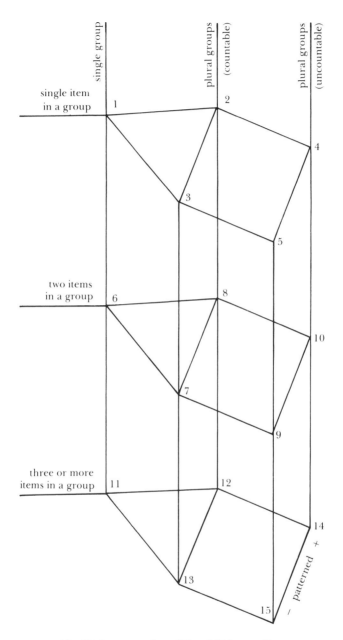

Fig. 17. Concatenation of Plural Objects at Rest

127

Plurality

In recent years much attention has been given to the different ways in which various languages label or categorize the color spectrum. Although hundreds of distinct points on the color spectrum are discernible by the naked human eye, languages classify the color spectrum into a small number of discrete categories, and these categories vary widely according to different languages.

Pitch is another area of human perception which is given various functions in the languages of the world. In some languages, such as Trique, as many as five levels of pitch are phonemic; in other languages, pitch functions only as a suprasegmental in the intonational system.

Number is another universal human perception. Number has not, however, received as much attention in linguistic and semantic studies as it probably deserves. Number is a linear continuum from zero to infinity. In cultures where mathematics is highly developed, minus numbers, fractions, and various other numerical values are distinguished by specialists. Languages indicate number in various ways. Most languages have a counting system according to which numbers from one to various amounts are labeled.

Beyond the counting system of a language, the grammar of a language indicates number in various ways. There are indefinite adjectives such as "a few," "some," and "many" in English, and *t'áá díkwíí'í, łá,* and *t'óó ahayóí* in Navajo. Number is also indicated by pronouns, nouns, and verbs. In English grammar number is divided into two basic categories: singular and plural. These two basic categories penetrate nearly the entire grammar. In subject pronouns there are "I" and "we," and "he" or "she" and "they." In demonstrative pronouns, there are "this" and "these," "that" and "those." In possessive pronouns, there are "mine" and "ours," and "his" or "hers" and "theirs." In nouns there are "bear" and "bears," "cat" and "cats," "man" and "men," etc. In cases such as deer and sheep, the plural is not marked. In verbs there are "he sits" and "they sit," but in the first person, number is indicated only by the subject pronoun. Number is not indicated at all in the second person.

Navajo grammar marks the number continuum in at least six different ways. These are:

(1) one / two / countable / uncountable

(2) one / two / three or more

(3) one / countable / uncountable

(4) countable (including one) / uncountable

(5) one or two / three or more

(6) one / two or more

The category labeled countable refers to a number of things that can easily be ascertained from a quick or short glance, whereas uncountable refers to a number of things so numerous that one cannot determine their exact number without taking the time to count them one by one. Thus countable is used here to refer to numbers normally less than ten, while uncountable at a glance refers to numbers more than ten and usually much greater than ten.

Navajo subject pronouns in the first and second persons signify number according to continuum (3) listed above. Subject pronouns in the third person signify only the two categories listed in continuum (4). Navajo subject pronouns are listed below:

	one	countable	uncountable
1st person	*shí*	*nihí*	*danihí*
2d person	*ní*	*nihí*	*danihí*
3d person	*bí*	*bí*	*daabí*

Navajo possessive pronouns signify number in the same way the subject pronouns do. The demonstrative pronouns of Navajo do not signify number and may refer to any number or amount.

Most Navajo nouns do not indicate number. Thus *dibé* can mean one sheep or many sheep. Some nouns, however, indicate number according to continuum (6) above:

ashkii / ashiiké
one boy / two or more boys

sitsóí / sitsóóké
my maternal grandchild / my maternal grandchildren

A few Navajo nouns[1] signify number according to continuum (4) above. Two examples of these are:

kǫ' / daakǫ'
one or several fires / many fires

ahi'diitiin / ahida'diitiin
several roads come together / many roads come together

Navajo verbs signify number according to continuums (1), (2), (3), or (5). An example of each is provided:

(1) to be standing (first person)
   sézį́ / siidzí / nisiidzí / ndasiidzí
   one / two / countable / uncountable

(2) to be walking along (first person)
   yishááł / yiit'ash / yiikah
   one / two / three or more

(3) a long or thin, rigid object at rest
   sitą́ / naaztą́ / ndaaztą́
   one / countable / uncountable

(5) to be (third person)
   nilį́ / danilį́
   one or two / three or more

Grouping

The next variable involved in Navajo categories of plural items at rest is grouping. Navajos categorize plural items according to whether they are considered separate and distinct or whether they are considered to constitute a group, according to whether they form just one group or many groups, and according to the number of items within each group. For example, a single pile (group) of a few logs is described as *tsin sinil*. Several piles (groups) of several logs would be described as *tsin naaznil*. If several logs were each lying separately they would be described as *tsin naaztá*, but if the same number of logs were in a pile (one group) they would be described as *tsin sinil*.

In the construction of a hogan there may be five to eight sides, each having ten or more logs. This can be described with the verb form *nínil*, meaning several groups of something with each group having several items within it.

A hundred sheep that are thought of as one herd (group) will be described as *dibé sijéé'*, but the same number of sheep considered as ungrouped entities will be described as *dibé ndaaztį*. If the speaker is considering the fact that each of the lambs is sitting with its mother, he will say *dibé biyázhí yił ndaazhtéézh*. In each case, the neuter verb is different because of the factor of grouping.

Patterning

Patterning or ordering is another conceptual distinction which is significant and pervasive in Navajo language and culture. In its pristine condition the first world was unordered and First Man and First Woman proceeded through the power of the word and the symbol to order things. Later, through means of witchcraft, this order was disturbed and disrupted, so that disorder occurred. Rituals came into being to reorder the disordered world. The polar positions of random, unordered things and patterned, ordered things seem to be associated with the terms *hózhǫ́* and *hóchxǫ'*, the former of which describes a beautiful, harmonious, and orderly environment and the latter of which describes an ugly, disharmonious, and disorderly environment.

Both order and disorder are first conceived in thought, and then projected on the world through speech and action. In both Navajo language and culture, things are considered to be in a random or an unordered condition unless a thinking, animate being has ordered them into some sort of a pattern.

Earlier in this section a three dimensional paradigm was presented as illustrating a Navajo conceptual scheme for categorizing plural items at rest. The paradigm contains fifteen basic categories for each general category. However, not every general category has fifteen distinct terms so that many conceptual categories are left unlabeled. Let us explore some of the terminology for several general categories.

The term *sizí* is applied to a single animate being in an erect position. If there are several distinct animate beings standing in a random distribution, the term *naazí* is used. If a similar number of animate objects in a standing position are in a pattern, the term *nízí* is used. The uncountable plural of *naazí* is *ndaazí,* and the countable plural of *nízí* is *danízí.* These five terms are the complete list of terms for animate beings in an erect position. The other ten categories on the paradigm remain unlabeled (see fig. 18). Actually the five terms on the top level are used to describe the corresponding categories on the two lower levels, so each of the five terms are polysemic and also label the ten lower categories.

A more complete set of terms can be found in the general category of animate beings in a sitting or semierect position. *Sidá* refers to one animate being in a sitting position. Several (countable) animate beings sitting in a separate and dispersed manner are described as *naazdá.* Several animate beings sitting in a pattern are described by the term *nídá.* The uncountable plurals of *naazdá* and *nídá* are *ndaazdá* and *danídá* respectively.

When there are two animate beings sitting together or in some way considered a group, the term *siké* is used. If there are several

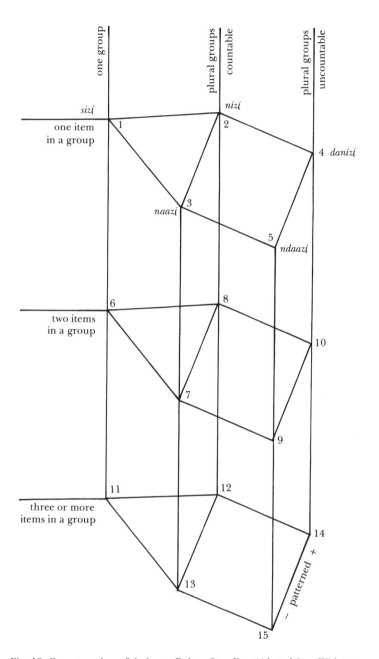

Fig. 18. Concatenation of Animate Beings Standing (*Adapted from Witherspoon, 1971:116*)

pairs of animate beings sitting in random distribution, *naazké* is the proper term. If several pairs of animate beings are sitting in a pattern, the term *níké* is used. The uncountable plural of *naazké* is *ndaazké,* and the uncountable plural of *níké* is *daníké.* Thus far we have ten of the fifteen categories labeled.

According to the categorical scheme, there should be a term for three or more animate beings sitting together or in a group, but no such term exists. It is interesting in this regard that in the active paradigm (this being the neuter or static paradigm) there is a term (*nibįįh*) that completes the paradigm. Here, however, there are only two terms for three or more animate beings sitting in a group. One is *naháaztą́* which means several groups sitting in random distribution. The other term is *ndaháaztą́* which means numerous (uncountable) groups (each made up of three or more) of animate beings sitting in a random distribution. *Naháaztą́* is used in reference to one group of three or more, but its prefix indicates its primary referent is several groups of three or more. Thus in this general category, twelve of the fifteen categories are labeled (see fig. 19).

A complete set of terms exists for the general category of an animate being or beings in a lying or nonerect position. The terms are shown in Figure 20. From this paradigm it can be seen that every conceptual category is labeled. If we look at the term *nítéézh,* we can see it means several (countable plural) pairs of animate beings lying in a pattern. If we go one category to the right, we get numerous pairs lying in a pattern. If we go one category downward from *nítéézh,* everything remains the same except that the groups made of two beings become three or more. If we come toward us to *naaztéézh,* we see that everything remains as it was with *nítéézh* save that patterning is lost and the distribution becomes random.

If we go to the left from *nítéézh* to *sitéézh,* the several groups of pairs become just one pair. The patterning is also lost because one pair cannot be in a pattern. If we go upwards from *nítéézh* to *nítį́* the only change is that the pairs in pattern become single beings in pattern. Thus the paradigm presented here illustrates the proper relationship between and among all the terms.

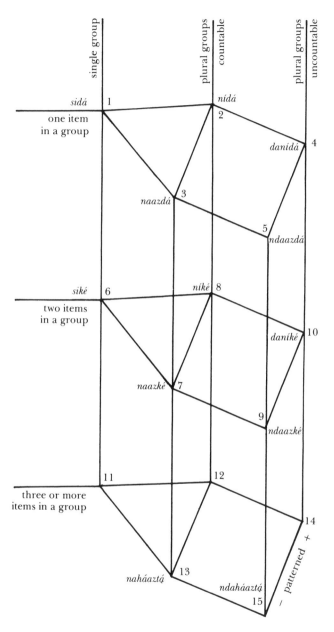

Fig. 19. Concatenation of Animate Beings Sitting (*Adapted from Witherspoon, 1971:117*)

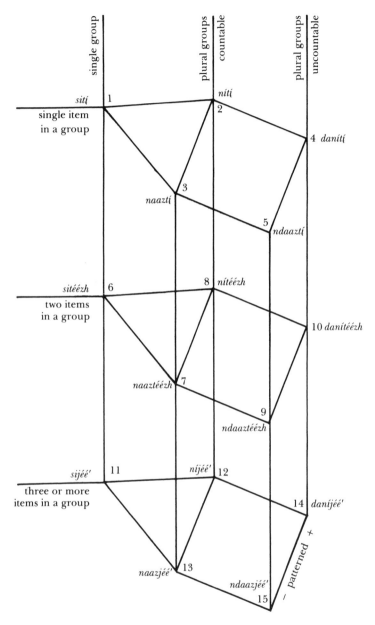

Fig. 20. Concatenation of Animate Beings Lying Down (*Adapted from Witherspoon,*
1971:118)

It should also be noted that there are two dimensions or con-
tinua of plurality utilized in this conceptual scheme. If we start at
the top left-hand corner with a single group and go across the
top, the number of groups becomes plural according to categories
of singular / countable / uncountable. If we go downwards from
the singular item, we see that the items within a group become
plural according to the scale of one / two / three or more. The
neuter verbs found here label the plural dimension of the number
of items within a group separately from the number of groups.
Trying to define the meaning of complex verbs according to only
one dimension of plurality has caused many students of Navajo to
misunderstand the correct referents of many Navajo verbs.

The conceptual scheme presented here is also applicable to the
other general categories of objects at rest. Although in most of the
object classifications there is an incomplete set of terms and many
categories are not labeled, there is one more category that is completely labeled. This set applies to houses or hogans and can be
very useful to the social anthropologist. (Fig. 21 shows the conceptual scheme for the classification of hogans or houses.) If a plural
number of hogans are considered as separate or unconnected, the
terms *naaz'ą́* or *ndaaz'ą́* are used. If several hogans are considered
as a group or unit, the term *sinil* is used. If there are two groups
of hogans, the term *naaznil* will be used. Because social units,
namely the "camp" or subsistence residential unit (Witherspoon,
1970:60), correspond to hogan groupings, the social anthropologist can determine what hogans represent a social unit or units by
the verbs which people use in describing them.

The term *kin sijaa'* refers to numerous houses in a group, which
means a town or a village. *Kin naazhjaa'* refers to several towns or
villages, and *kin ndaazhjaa'* refers to numerous towns or villages.
Hoghan sinil refers to one camp; *hoghan naaznil* refers to several
camps. *Hoghan si'ą́* refers to one household; *hoghan naaz'ą́* refers
to several households.

The camp or subsistence residential unit is built around a sheep
herd. If in a particular area the ethnographer hears the phrase
kojí dibé sijéé' he will know there is just one herd of sheep and one

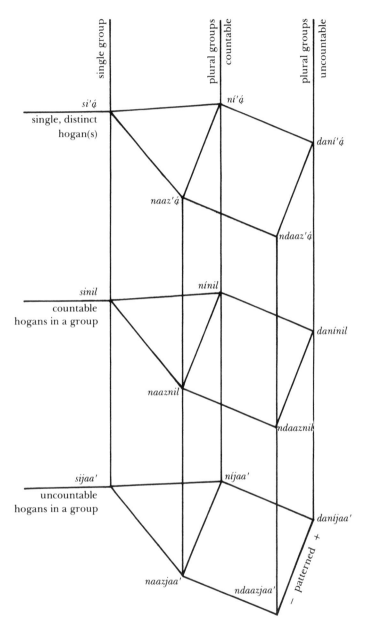

Fig. 21. Concatenation of Inanimate Items at Rest (*Adapted from Witherspoon, 1971:120*)

138

camp. However, if the term used is *kojí dibé naazjéé'*, the ethnographer can be sure there is more than one sheep herd and thus more than one camp.

The examples, paradigms, and discussions above illustrate how the domain of objects at rest is partitioned and concatenated in the Navajo world. It was shown that the fifteen general categories, which are ostensibly based on such variables as animateness, shape, size, and degree of containment, cohesiveness, or rigidity, are actually partitioned on the basis of the ability or potential of an item or entity to move or be moved. Within each of the fifteen general classes, the variables of plurality, grouping, and patterning intersect to create and define fifteen additional categories according to which speakers of Navajo discriminate and signify objects at rest, making a total of 225 categories. Many of these categories, however, are not labeled by distinct terms, for some terms label more than one category. As I reported in an earlier paper on this subject (1971), the Navajo language provides 102 distinct monolexical labels for objects at rest. This number, 102, seems at first to be totally arbitrary, but a wider and deeper cultural perspective questions the arbitrariness of this number.

In the emergence myth of the Upward Reaching Way, it is reported that there are 102 roads of life. In another myth Turquoise Boy asked to have 102 trails to follow (O'Bryan, 1956:18). Elsewhere in discussing the pathways of the sun, the inner form of the sun states: "I have 102 roads and that number of people will die" (Goddard, 1933:135). This seems to be based on the idea that the sun moves in a cycle of 102 phases, and that the proper age to die is 102. Reichard notes that "a large and explainable even number is the reference to 102 years as the age of man— probably the ideal of a long life span" (1950a:243). Here, it seems, we find that not only do the 102 terms for objects at rest classify objects on the basis of their ability or potential to move or to be moved, but that even this number of terms seems to be unmistakably related to the way according to which man harmonizes his life movements with the cosmic order found in the pathways of the sun.

From the foregoing discussions and analyses we can again see how the perspective or dimension of movement dominates and pervades the Navajo view and classification of the world. The Navajo world is a world of motion—a world of action in which all beings and entities are either acting or being acted upon; a world of change in which both individual entities and systems are constantly going through phased cycles and processes of deformation and restoration; a world of things in motion and things at rest, but one in which even things at rest are defined by the withdrawal of motion and are classified according to their ability or potential to move or to be moved.

IV. CLASSIFYING SEX, DIRECTION, AND COLOR

Gender is a major attribute by which beings and entities in the Navajo world are differentiated and classified. Not only do all kinds of plant and animal species come in male and female varieties, but other things such as rain, mountains, ceremonies, hogans, directions, and so on also come in male and female varieties. Gender was an inherent attribute of the primordial creatures that inhabited the first world:

> The First World, Ni'hodilqil, was black as black wool. It had four corners, and over these appeared four clouds. These four clouds contained within themselves the elements of the First World. They were in color, black, white, blue, and yellow. . . .
>
> In the East, at the place where the Black Cloud and the White Cloud met, First Man, Atse'hastqin, was formed. . . .
>
> Now on the western side of the First World . . . there appeared the Blue Cloud, and opposite it there appeared the Yellow Cloud. Where they came together First Woman was formed . . . (O'Bryan, 1956:1–2).

Every Navajo who tells this story insists that thes‹
Man and First Woman, were humanlike only in tl
male and female and were attracted to each other.
pairs of colors from which First Man and First Wom
being—black and white for First Man and yellow
First Woman—constitute the mother and father of First Man and
First Woman respectively. This mixing of the colored clouds or
air masses represents the first conjugal union of the sexes, and the
offspring of the union of the sexes represent the first fruits or
results of sexual reproduction. One account of the creation story
explicitly likens this union to sexual intercourse:

> In the beginning there were only mists. There was no world
> then, only the white, yellow, blue, black, silver, and red mists
> floating in the air. The mists came together and laid on top
> of each other, like intercourse (Fishler, 1953:9).

It was from these early mist people, creatures of the air, made of
color (light) and mist (air and water), that evolved all the species
found in this, the fifth world.

Male beings in the Navajo world are characterized by a number
of associated traits, and these traits are paired with, but opposite
to, traits characteristic of female beings. Maleness is associated
with the static dimension of reality, while femaleness is associated
with the active dimension of reality. In the Navajo view, it is the
female who is active, productive, and reproductive. The capacity
to create or reproduce life and propagate the species is inherent
in the female, and the capacity to sustain life and produce food is
associated with the female. The earth and its life-giving, life-sus-
taining, and life-producing qualities are associated with and derived from Changing Woman. It is not surprising, therefore, that
women tend to dominate in social and economic affairs. Women
are the heads of most domestic groups, the clans are matrilineal,
and the land and sheep traditionally were controlled by the
women of the residential groups.

Sạ'ah Naagháii ("thought") is male and *Bik'eh Hózhǫ́* ("speech") is female (cf. page 17). Thought is the inner form and speech is the outer form. Thought is associated with the static dimension of reality, and speech is associated with the active dimension of reality. The ritual or ceremonial domain of Navajo culture is associated with thought and with the male. Most ceremonial practitioners are men. The ceremonies are rigidly and statically structured. They never change and are effective only when they are performed without mistakes or modifications. On the other hand, Navajo social and economic life is characterized by movement and change, activity and productivity, and thus it seems appropriate that women would dominate in this sphere of Navajo life and culture. Navajo ceremonies are primarily concerned with the restoration of prior states of being, whereas Navajo social and economic life is primarily concerned with the generation of new conditions and new beings wherein fertility and fecundity, productivity and reproductivity are especially important.

As the inner form, the male is associated with the origin and culmination of things, whereas the female, the outer form, is associated with growth, process, and change. This is expressed in a number of Navajo classificatory schemes. East, the beginning point of the day and all directional sequences, is male, and north, the culminating point of the daily path of the sun (associated with night and darkness) and the concluding point in all directional sequences, is also male. In the daily pathway of the sun, south is the second point and is associated with daylight, and west is associated with the evening twilight. Both of these latter cardinal directions are female. These associations of gender, direction, and the daily path of the sun are summarized:

male: east: dawn
female: south: daylight
female: west: twilight
male: north: night.

This process and sequence is also expressed in other conceptual formulations. The sky is male and the earth is female. Water (associated with semen and the male) comes down from the sky to the earth, then growth occurs from the earth upward toward the sky (Reichard, 1950a:162). As this growth reaches upward it matures and eventually dies. Thus while the male is associated with the origin and culmination of life, the female is associated with the generation and growth of life. The cycle of life is linked with the path of the sun in Navajo thought by the association of death and the dead with the north, the male and the static dimension of reality. In contrast the daytime and the earth are associated with activity and productivity.

This same set of conceptual associations and related processes is found in the four-phased cycle of the year. The spring represents the birth or beginning of life, the summer represents the growth of life, the fall represents the maturing of life, and the winter represents the death or decay of life. These also follow the male-female-female-male conceptual pattern or sequence. The circular or cyclical process expressed in the above conceptual paradigms begins by going from inner form (male) to outer form (female) and concludes by going from outer form (female) to inner form (male). This sort of balanced inversion seems to be characteristic of Navajo thought (Reichard, 1944:5) and Navajo language (cf. chapter 3, section I). This process also expresses the dualistic transformation of the static state into the active state and then the return of the active state to the static state, prepared for another activation.

The emphasis and value that the Navajo place on the active dimension—life and movement—are also found in the Navajo beliefs that daytime and light are good and beautiful, whereas nighttime and darkness are lacking in beauty and are dangerous and potentially evil. Thus normally Navajos are active in the daytime and static at night. The exception to this pattern occurs when the normal order has been disrupted and reversed—*hóchxǫ'* has replaced *hózhǫ́*. In this case of reversal, Navajos must be active at night in ritual activities to restore the world to its normal and desirable condition wherein many good things happen in the daytime and little or nothing happens at night.

Another reversal of this normal and desirable pattern is found in the nighttime activities of witches. Witches are active when one should be static and static when one should be active. Thus witches initiate a process that begins by going from the active to the static, and to reverse this process medicine men must take the patient from his static condition to an active one. This final stage or process completes the inverted cycles, exorcises the evil from the patient, and returns the evil to the abnormal one who set it in inverted motion.

Color

For the Navajo color is the symbolic base for another language. Color is considered to be a dimension of light. Reichard notes this view of color as an attribute of light:

> Though the Navaho are so impressed by color that they have woven it into their entire ritualistic scheme, they seem to regard it as a function of light. In Stevenson's origin myth we are told, "By the time they had reached the fourth world the people had separated light into its several colors" (Stevenson, 1886:275; quoted in Reichard, 1950a:250).

The underworlds had no sun and were lighted only by single or individual colors. The first world was the darkest, and its color was black. The color of the second world was blue, the color of the third world was yellow, and the color of the fourth world was red. In the present fifth world, the sun combines all the colors of the underworlds into the light of daytime. Nighttime, being without sunlight, is symbolic of a return to the darkness and chaotic but formative conditions of the underworld. Thus ritual drama—which begins with a return to the underworlds and a reenactment of the undesirable events and resulting conditions found in episodes of cultural heroes and concludes with a triumphant restoration of *hózhǫ́* and a glorious reemergence to the beautiful, color-, cosmos of the fifth world—appropriately begins during t and culminates with the healed patient going to ng sun.

Light, like sound, is closely associated with air, and color, like pitch with regard to sound, seems to be an inherent quality or attribute of light. The air masses which joined to create the mist beings or wind souls of the first world were each of a specific color, and all wind souls found in beings of the fifth world are colored. Light, like sound, is also transmitted through the air. It is sunlight which combines all colors in its brilliance and also makes the colors of all things visible. Darkness destroys or eliminates all sense or perception of color, and is thus a kind of noncommunicative silence.

Individual colors or pigments may be considered the phonemes or pigmemes (to coin a word) of the Navajo language of light. In this language blue and yellow seem to have a vocalic nature or role, while black, white, red, variegated, and so on appear to parallel the role of consonants in language. The reason I refer to colors as pigmemes in this language is that they do not, for the most part, separately or individually mean or signify anything. These colors take on symbolic meaning in connection with or in contrast to other colors in a pair or in a sequence. The language of light or color seems to possess a definite syntax, and its meanings can only be understood when one understands the rules of its syntax.

From interpretations and analyses of color symbolism in many cultures, one gets the impression that individual colors express constant meanings. For the Navajo this pattern is simply not true. In one context white may signify maleness; in another context it may signify femaleness. This is also true for black, yellow, and most of the other colors. In addition, white may signify east in one context and north in another. The same is true for black. The links between colors and directions and colors and gender are not constant and must be determined from the context and sequence in which they are found.

The symbolic link between color and direction is more definite and constant than the symbolic link between color and gender. There is a standard color sequence for the cardinal directions: white for east, blue[2] for south, yellow for west, and black for north. If we add this set of colors to the conceptual associations listed earlier, we get the following result:

white: male: east: dawn
blue: female: south: daylight
yellow: female: west: twilight
black: male: north: night.

In reading this set of colors, it should be noted that although the sequence goes from east to south to west to north, the paired directions are east and west and south and north. In either case the patterns go from male to female and female to male.

A variation of the standard color sequence is black-blue-yellow-white. Haile believes that the use of this color sequence is reason for suspecting that witchcraft may be involved:

The colored winds, too, which are assigned in proper sequence to the phenomena of the cardinal points, to wit: white wind soul to dawn, blue wind soul to horizontal blue, yellow wind soul to evening twilight, dark wind soul to darkness, are considered benevolent, if mentioned in this sequence in religious functions. But when a ceremonial, in its songs and prayers, disturbs this sequence, giving preference to darkness, malevolence and witchery may be suspected (Haile, 1943:75).

Although what Haile suggests above may be true in some cases, it is not necessarily true. Black is not only a symbol of evil and danger; it also protects one from evil and danger. This, of course, is the basis of the Navajo theory behind the blackening rite in which the patient is covered with black ashes and tallow. The main purpose of this rite is to disguise the patient and make him invisible to evil ghosts who would do him harm. Reichard believes that if the rite starts out with dangerous episodes, the patient needs to start with the color black to give him some initial protection he may need while making ritual contact with dangerous entities or malevolent beings (1950a:222).

The most significant question for an analysis of color symbolism is whether black in the color sequence black-blue-yellow-white becomes a symbol of east or whether the sequence starts in the north. Reichard assumes the former explanation is correct:

> The most frequent sequence not fully accounted for by the rules of sex and sequence is *b-u-y-w*. The difference between it and the one just discussed is that the colors of the north and east change places (1950a:221).

I suspect that in at least some cases, the sequence black-blue-yellow-white does not involve any transposing of colors for directions, but that the directional sequence reverses the normal order and goes from north to south and then west to east. In either case, the sex sequence is not disturbed because both white and black are male colors.

It is interesting to note that red, pink, and variegated are sometimes substituted for black in the four-colored sequence. In all such cases, however, white remains the first color in the sequence, while the substitute for black is always the last color in the sequence. This illustrates that a color acquires its symbolic meaning and value, in many instances, not from its constant link with a particular meaning, but from its place in a particular sequence.

Although blue is always in the south and is usually female, in the Shooting Chant it is male. When blue is paired with and thus contrasted to black, blue is always female and black is always male. But in the Shooting Chant blue is paired with yellow. Here blue is male and yellow is female. When white is paired with blue or yellow, it is always male. But when white is paired with black as in the case of the Shooting Chant, white is female and black is male. Yellow is always female in contrast to black and white but it can be male in contrast to blue. For example, there is a Horizontal Blue Girl who is often paired with a Horizontal Yellow Boy. Nevertheless, as I pointed out above, in the Shooting Chant yellow is female and blue is male.

A careful analysis of the symbolic associations of sex and color indicates that yellow is always female when contrasted to black or white, and that black and white are always male when paired with either yellow or blue. Ambiguity arises when blue and yellow (usually both female colors) are contrasted with each other or when white and black (usually both male colors) are contrasted with each other. In an attempt to understand this ambiguity or apparent paradox, one must go back to the story of events occurring in the first world. Here we find that:

> The Black Cloud represented the Female Being or Substance. For as a child sleeps when being nursed, so life slept in the darkness of the Female Being. The White Cloud represented the Male Being or Substance. . . .

> In the east, at the place where the Black Cloud and the White Cloud met, First Man, Atse'hastqin, was formed . . . (O'Bryan, 1956:1).

Here we see that a female color, black, and a male color, white, joined to form First Man. Similarly First Woman evolved from a union of a blue and a yellow cloud, in which case the blue cloud represents the male and the yellow cloud represents the female. But in contrast to black and white, blue and yellow are both linked to First Woman and are thus female. The analysis here might best be seen in the form of a taxonomy as illustrated in figure 22. In the Shooting Chant and in a few other contexts, the white and blue found on the lowest level of this taxonomy are interposed. This also occurs to blue and yellow on the same level. But there is no interposing of the sex-linked meanings of these colors at the higher level of the taxonomy. There white and black are always male in contrast to blue and yellow which are always female. Thus the Navajo language of color or light illustrates a pattern of polysemy similar to that found in the analysis of *k'é* terms, and the use of inversion found in the analysis of Navajo syntax also seems to be operating in patterns of color sequence or syntax.

In the Shooting Chant, white is at the east and is female, while blue is at the south and is male. Accordingly, yellow is at the west and is female, while black is at the north and is male. This in-

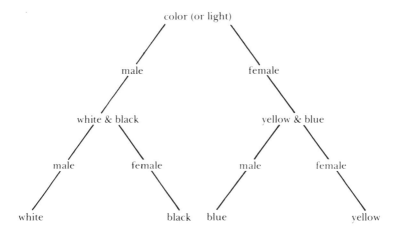

Fig. 22. Taxonomy of Color Categories

verted view or classification of color and sex is based on the same distinctions of static/active and male/female as the more standard view which has white as male and blue as female. This inverted view seems to be based on the observation that dawn and twilight are really active times of the day, involving a fast-moving transition from one state to a different state. Daytime and nighttime, however, are both somewhat static, in contrast to dawn and twilight which are in transition. From this viewpoint, east and west are appropriately classified as female, while south and north are appropriately classified as male.

The most important point of this section of chapter 3 is that the patterns of classification of sex, direction, and color also reflect the basic metaphysical distinction between the static and active dimensions of reality. In previous sections it has been shown how this basic distinction has provided an organizing principle upon which much of the linguistic classification of the world is built. In this section we found that the language of light, utilizing color for its pigmemes or symbols, illustrates many of the same semantic features and patterns found in the phonetically based language. Therefore, regardless of the symbolic base utilized, the Navajo linguistic classification of the world is built upon the same metaphysical assumptions and oppositions.

CHAPTER 4

Beautifying the World through Art

In the Western world, where mind has been separated from body, where man has been extracted from nature, where affect has been divorced from "fact," where the quest for and focus upon the manipulation and accumulation of things has led man to exploit rather than to respect and admire the earth and her web of life, it is not surprising that art would be divorced from the more practical affairs of business and government and the more serious matters of science, philosophy, and theology. In the Navajo world, however, art is not divorced from everyday life, for the creation of beauty and the incorporation of oneself in beauty represent the highest attainment and ultimate destiny of man. *Hózhǫ́* expresses the Navajo concept of beauty or beautiful conditions. But beauty is not separated from good, from health, from happiness, or from harmony. Beauty—*hózhǫ́*—is the combination of all these conditions. It is not an abstractable quality of things or a fragment of experience; it is the normal pattern of nature and the most desirable form of experience.

For the Navajo, beauty is not so much in the eye of the beholder as it is in the mind of its creator and in the creator's relationship to the created (that is, the transformed or the organized). The Navajo does not look for beauty; he generates it within himself and projects it onto the universe. The Navajo says *shił hózhǫ́* 'with me there is beauty', *shii' hózhǫ́* 'in me there is beauty', and *shaa hózhǫ́* 'from me beauty radiates'. Beauty is not "out there" in things to be perceived by the perceptive and appreciative viewer; it is a creation of thought. The Navajo experience beauty primarily through expression and creation, not through perception and preservation. Beauty is not so much a perceptual experience as it is a conceptual one.

In the Western world beauty as a quality of things to be per-

ceived is, in essence, static; that is, it is something to be observed
and preserved. To the Navajo, however, beauty is an essential
condition of man's life and is dynamic. It is not in things so much
as it is in the dynamic relationships among things and between
man and things. Man experiences beauty by creating it. For the
Anglo observer of Navajo sandpaintings, it has always been a
source of some bewilderment and frustration that the Navajo "de-
stroy" these sandpaintings in less time than they take to create
them. To avoid this overt destruction of beauty and to preserve its
artistic value, the Anglo observer always wants to take a photo-
graph of the sandpainting, but the Navajo sees no sense and some
danger in that. To the Navajo the artistic or aesthetic value of the
sandpainting is found in its creation, not in its preservation. Its
ritual value is in its symbolic or representational power and in its
use as a vehicle of conception. Once it has served that purpose, it
no longer has any ritual value.

    Navajos take little interest in the display or preservation of their
works of art, with the exception of silver and turquoise jewelry.
They readily sell them to non-Indians who are looking for beauty
in things. Traditionally, they put their works of art to practical use
in their daily activities. Now it is more practical to sell them for
money and buy stainless steel pots and other more durable but
less artistic things. This practice offends the purist's view of aesthetics, but it is, in fact, not a depreciation of aesthetic value at all.
It is simply based on the idea that beauty is a dynamic experience
in conception and expression, not a static quality of things to be
perceived and preserved.

    With regard to the two different views of art contrasted above, it
is not surprising that Navajo society is one of artists (art creators)
while Anglo society consists primarily of nonartists who view art
(art consumers). The Navajo find it incomprehensible that we have
more art critics than we have artists, and more art collectors than
we have art creators. Nearly all Navajos are artists and spend a
large part of their time in artistic creation. All Navajos are singers,
and most Navajos have composed many songs. Traditionally, over
90 percent of all adult women wove rugs and today, despite limited

opportunities to learn this art, a majority of Navajo women over thirty still weave. A large number of Navajo men are skilled at silver work and sandpainting. Some women still make pottery and beautifully designed baskets. Teachers in Navajo schools find that nearly all Navajo students take a special interest in and have an unusual proficiency in the graphic arts. Navajos are also very eloquent and often poetic in their use of language.

In white society it is the exceptional and abnormal person that becomes an artist. The artist is usually associated with marginality and nonconformity with regard to the mainstream of society. From this marginal position the artist dedicates himself almost solely to his artistic creations. The nonartist among the Navajo is a rarity. Moreover, Navajo artists integrate their artistic endeavors into their other activities. Living is not a way of art for them, but art is a way of living.

Navajo artistic interests and talents are enhanced by, if not derived from, the emphasis on the creative nature of thought and the compulsive power of speech. Art is a nondiscursive form of expression, but it involves many of the same processes of symbolic transformation that are found in discursive symbolism. Professor A. D. Richie has noted that "the essential act of thought is symbolization" (1936:279), and art is as much symbolization as is speech. Art is a symbolic transformation of experience, and, as such, it invests and imbues experience—thus life—with beauty and aesthetic value and meaning.

Navajo culture is not just a food-gathering strategy; it is an artistic way of life. One is admonished to walk in beauty, speak in beauty, act in beauty, sing in beauty, and live in beauty. All things are to be made beautifully, and all activities are to be completed in beauty. The following daily prayer exemplifies the Navajo emphasis on beauty:

> With beauty before me, I walk
> With beauty behind me, I walk
> With beauty above me, I walk
> With beauty below me, I walk

From the East beauty has been restored
From the South beauty has been restored
From the West beauty has been restored
From the North beauty has been restored
From the zenith in the sky beauty has been restored
From the nadir of the earth beauty has been restored
From all around me beauty has been restored.

The separation of mind and body—or, in the popular idiom, mind and heart—in Western metaphysics has led aesthetic analysis and interpretation into confusion as to what it is that the artist expresses in his work. Experience is divided into fragments which relate to the intellectual realm, the emotional realm, and the aesthetic realm. A major question, then, is whether a particular art work expresses an "idea," whether it expresses the emotions and feelings of the artist who created it, or whether it expresses nothing in the way of ideas or emotions, and simply possesses significant and aesthetic form, a pure expression of beauty.

In the Navajo world, where mind and matter, thought and expression are inseparably connected, the aesthetic experience—the creation of beauty—is simultaneously intellectual, emotional, moral, aesthetic, and biological. Navajo life and culture are based on a unity of experience, and the goal of Navajo life—the creation, maintenance, and restoration of *hózhǫ*—expresses that unity of experience. *Hózhǫ* expresses the intellectual concept of order, the emotional state of happiness, the moral notion of good, the biological condition of health and well-being, and the aesthetic dimensions of balance, harmony, and beauty. In Navajo art we find all these concepts, states, and conditions expressed.

As the essence of the Navajo conception of life is movement or motion, and the experience of beauty is dynamic and flowing, characteristic themes found in Navajo art express this emphasis on movement and activity. In *Philosophy in a New Key* (1957:226–27), Suzanne Langer quotes Jean D'Udine's description of music:

    . . . "all music is dancing. . . . Every feeling contributes, in
    effect, certain special gestures which reveal to us, bit by bit,

the essential characteristic of Life: movement. . . . All living creatures are constantly consummating their own internal rhythm." . . . And these rhythms are the prototypes of musical structures, for all art is but a projection of them from one domain of sense to another, a symbolic transformation. "Every artist is a transformer; all artistic creation is but a transmutation."

A Navajo often counts his wealth in the songs he knows and especially in the songs he has created. A poor Navajo is one who has no songs, for songs enrich one's experiences and beautify one's activities. Songs accompany and enrich both ceremonial and nonceremonial activities. There are riding songs, walking songs, grinding songs, planting songs, growing songs, and harvesting songs. There are songs to greet the sun in the morning and songs to bid it farewell in the evening. There are songs for horses, for sheep, and for various other animal species. There are songs for blessing a hogan and songs for taking a sweat bath. In the past there were even songs for bidding visitors farewell. And, of course, there are songs of love and romance. But the most powerful songs are those that are essential parts of ceremonial and ritual activities. The former type is a means by which Navajos maintain *hózhǫ́* in their daily life experiences, while the latter type constitutes a means by which Navajos restore *hózhǫ́* when it has been disrupted.

Professor David McAllester, who has spent over twenty-five years studying Navajo music, says Navajo music is characterized by its vigor, its power, and its acrobatic style. It is intense, at times almost "excessive," compared to Pueblo music which is low, controlled, and rehearsed. Navajo music seems to match the cultural emphasis on energy, activity, and motion. There is hardly ever a "held" note, except at the end of a song (McAllester, personal correspondence).

In analyzing the First Snake Song, Professor McAllester finds that one of its chief characteristics is repetition. Repetition is a motif found all through Navajo life and culture. It is associated with the concepts of renewal, regeneration, rejuvenation, revolution, and restoration. Repetition enhances the compulsive power of the song. The repetitive nature of many Navajo songs is adorned with and enlivened by various modes of variation:

If we are to consider repetition and the values associated with it as a cognitive theme running through Navajo life and exemplified in the First Snake Song, this is not to say that this song, or Navajo music in general, is simple, childlike or boring. Navajos do not find it so, nor would any outsider who penetrates far enough into the material, either stylistically or ideationally, to see the subtle and constant variations ... such modes of variation as interruption, alternation, return, pairing, progression, transection, and ambiguity. These may be seen as contrapuntal to the theme of repetition (McAllester, n.d.:12).

In the First Snake Song there is a significant alternation in the *kind* of melodic activity. This is found between level sections based entirely or largely on the tonic, and active sections characterized by rapid and pulsing movement. McAllester considers this to be the quality in Navajo "chanting" that makes the term a misnomer (n.d.:16).

The verses of the First Snake Song also exhibit the principle of alternation. Here there are found alternations in colors, in sex, in directions, and in jewel symbols. This is a way of presenting pairs of related objects:

The text reinforces the concept so persistently stated by musical means. Four sacred personages are involved in this brief poem, carrying a big snake that becomes a big hoop. There are two male protagonists and two who are female. Transecting this complementarity is another: maturity and immaturity. A special aspect of this duality is a shifting back and forth between the sexes, an expression of their complementarity. This is stated mythically in the reconciliation that was necessary after the separation of the sexes. It is also stated in the constant care exercised to include both sexes in ritual acts and to see to it that the male and female sides of the various entities are represented as in Changing Woman's other side, represented by White Shell Woman, and Enemy Slayer's other side represented by Child Born for Water. In the Holy Family in Shootingway, the idea is carried even farther: a "Quaternity" is represented of four persons in one, and even four sexes, two adult and two immature. Reichard (1939:15) identifies this as the "principle of multiple selves" (McAllester, n.d.:19).

McAllester notes that although the First Snake Song is strophic and framed, it is progressive in that the pitch gradually rises from one song to the next. He relates this progression in pitch to a progression in textually expressed ideas where the movement is from mature male to immature female, from animate snake to inanimate hoop, from "holding," "dangling," "lugging" to "trundling" (n.d.:20–21). As noted earlier (cf. p. 143) maturity is often thought of as a static and thus male-linked condition, whereas immaturity is associated with activity, process, and growth and is female-linked in the Navajo metaphor. Since the animate snake is obviously active and the inanimate hoop is static, the progression here seems to go from static to active and from active to static. This is contrasted by the progression of "holding," "dangling," "lugging," and "trundling," which starts from the static "holding" and gets progressively more active.

In the actual performance of the First Snake Song, the musical principles of repetition, alternation, and progression, and the ideas associated with them, operate simultaneously and thus transect each other. "A repetition of duple rhythmic figures may be interrupted by a sequence in threes and at the same time a tension between prosodic and poetic text may be underway. A male-female alternation may be proceeding at one speed and a mature-immature alternation may transect this sequence, so to speak, at another speed" (McAllester, n.d.:24). McAllester represents these transections with the diagram shown in figure 23.

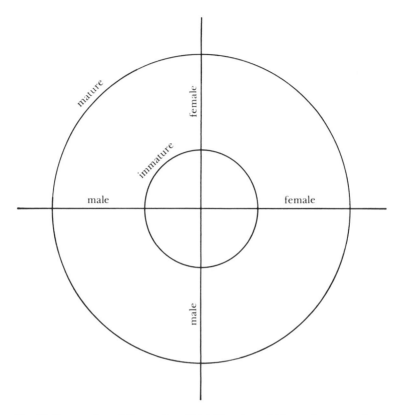

Fig. 23. Intersection of Categories of Male/Female and Mature/Immature (*From McAllester, n.d.:24*)

It seems to me that underlying this diagram is one in which static could be substituted for male and mature, and active could be substituted for female and immature. Also, by simply inverting the positions of male and female, one can see the Navajo pattern of the cardinal directions in the pathway of the sun. Likewise, if we relate the mature outer circle to the male sky and the immature—growing, changing, active—inner ring to the female earth, we can see the pattern of growth—rain (associated with semen) coming down to the earth, and then active, immature growth ascending upward to the mature and static condition again (fig. 24). In all cases, it seems to me, the initial sequence goes from static to active and the concluding sequence, which completes the cycle or revolution, goes from active to static.

The First Snake Song is just one part of the Snake Song complex, and the Snake Song is just one small part of the Shootingway ceremonial, which is just one of the more than half a hundred major ceremonies of the Navajo. McAllester concludes his analysis of this song with this comment: "In all the rich ceremo-

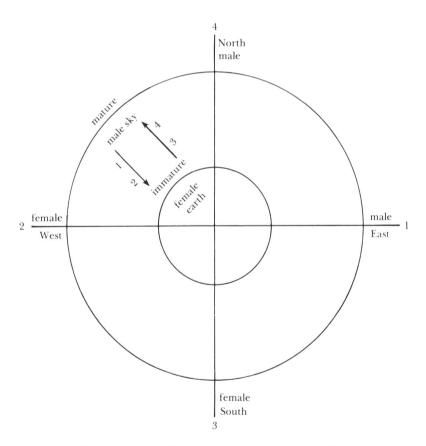

Fig. 24. Intersection of Categories of Sex, Maturity, and Direction

nial complex, the First Snake Song is merely one brief ritual communication. Yet in that small compass of music and poetry I hope to have suggested that some of the basic principles governing Navajo art and thought may be discerned" (n.d.:37).

Where Navajo music, singing, and poetry are artistic endeavors common to both men and women, the other two major domains of Navajo aesthetics, weaving and sandpainting, are sexually bifurcated. Weaving is primarily an activity of women,[1] and sandpainting is primarily an activity of men. Some Navajo men weave, but this associates them with the category of *nádlééhí*, 'transvestite'. Such a person, however, is usually held in high esteem and is not normally the object of ridicule or unkind behavior. Reichard notes that Left-Handed Singer of Newcomb was a man who wove. She states that he was highly respected, and a person of superior intelligence combined with extreme gentleness and remarkable independence. As an accomplished singer or "medicine man," he wove primarily sandpainting tapestries (1968:161). Sandpainting is exclusively a male activity. Even female singers do not do sandpainting, although they may supervise the creation of a sandpainting.

It is relevant to note that the composition and design of Navajo sandpaintings are static; that is, the designs are rigidly established and must be created without significant change or alteration if they are to be an effective part of the particular ritual for which they are used. In contrast, a weaver seldom if ever repeats a design. Each rug woven is designed anew, so designs are always changing, flowing, and moving. Thus the production of design in sandpainting and weaving seems to be appropriately associated with the generally static nature of male-linked endeavors and the dynamic nature of female-linked endeavors.

Before mass-produced retail goods became available to the Navajo, they had to produce their own blankets, garments, and moccasins. Although buckskin and other skins provided the raw materials to satisfy many of these needs, wool from sheep provided the major source of material for clothing and blankets. However, instead of just producing clothing and blankets to satisfy the pragmatic needs of warmth and protection from the elements, Navajo women turned the production of clothing and blankets into an artistic endeavor. Today, Navajo women weave rugs primarily for the use of non-Indians. Although they sell these rugs for cash, it has been estimated that the average weaver gets less than a quarter an hour for her work. Obviously, then, the motivation to weave is aesthetic as well as economic—probably even primarily aesthetic. Weaving is an effort in creative transformation. Navajo women transform the wool on the backs of sheep into beautifully designed and delicately woven rugs. This is done through the processes of shearing, cleaning, dyeing, carding, spinning, and weaving. Additional color is added through vegetal dyes.[2]

Navajo women develop and create designs in their minds, and then project them onto the world of external reality through the art of weaving. The intricate and often complex patterns created by Navajo weavers are generated in the mind and kept there through the whole process from dyeing through weaving. She must know exactly how much dye to use or exactly what amounts of black and white wool to mix in order to get the very exact color combinations and contrasts she has in her mind. In carrying out the design on the loom, she must keep the design in her mind in two ways:

The weaver must keep the composition of the entire rug surface in her mind, but she must see it as a huge succession of stripes only one weft strand wide. It matters not how ideal her general conception may be, if she cannot see it in terms of the narrowest stripe, meaning a row, of properly placed wefts, it will fail of execution (Reichard, 1968:86).

This is what is necessary for the weaver to maintain control of her composition, and to carry it out effectively. Weaving thus requires a unique combination and coordination of conceptual and manual skills. A woven rug is a product of the mind and the body. The inner form of the rug is in the mind; the outer form of the rug is projected onto the loom.

The emphasis on the creative nature of thought seems to encourage and enable Navajos to accomplish amazing mental feats. A singer memorizes, word for word, line for line, detailed prayers and songs that in some cases take nine days to perform. This is coupled with exact knowledge of ritual and mythical details, symbolic elements and costumes, and all the specifics and sequences of the dramatic behavior associated with the rite, plus all the details of the composition, design, and proportions of the one or several sandpaintings associated with the rite. Likewise, the Navajo weaver illustrates tremendous mental creativity and conceptual skills:

> Until quite recently the Navajo women wove all compositions "out of their heads." Most of them still do. That is, they visualize a design and carry it out. Some like Atlnaba, sure of plan and confident of skill, execute the initial conception unfalteringly (Reichard, 1968:112).

Reichard admits, however, that in her attempts to learn how to weave, she had to make a drawing of her design (1968:113).

In the patterns found on Navajo rugs, movement and activity are expressed by diagonal and zigzag lines (also associated with lightning), by the active colors of yellow (brown), blue (green), and red (pink), by appendages to various "static" centers, and by diamond shapes. In contrast, a static condition is expressed by straight lines and horizontal and vertical stripes, by squares and rectangles, and by the static colors of white, black, and grey. Motion goes in one of two directions: linear, continuative, incomplete motion, or circular, repetitious, complete, cyclical motion. In Navajo language the former is found in the important and extensively used imperfective and progressive modes and in the continuative aspect of Navajo verbs, while the latter is found in iterative and usitive modes and in the repetitive aspect of Navajo verbs. In addition linear and continuative motion is expressed by the verbal prefix *hi* which renders the idea of succession, while circular and repetitious actions and movements are expressed by the verbal prefixes *náá* and *ná* which express the ideas of repetition, revolution, and restoration (cf. pp. 21–22).

In the language of Navajo weaving, linear, continuative, and incomplete motion is expressed by the successive alternation of static and active symbols—colors, lines, and designs. Linear movement thus follows the pattern or series of static-active-static-active. Circular and cyclical movement is expressed by the sequence already noted: static-active-active-static. This pattern is found in the sequence of color, direction, and growth, and in the daily and annual path of the sun. It is sunwise motion. There is also an opposite sequence, usually associated with witchcraft and its cure, but also associated with protection and with an emphasis on activity, that goes from active to static and static to active (cf. pp. 146–49). The former type of cyclical movement is mainly found in Navajo ritual where control and normality are emphasized, whereas the latter type of cyclical movement is often found in Navajo weaving and other art forms where creativity and activity are emphasized.

Plates 1 through 5 are examples of blankets woven in the nineteenth century. These blankets represent Navajo weaving when it was in its late formative stage and before white traders started to have a significant influence on the types of designs woven in particular areas of the reservation. Plate 6 is a more modern example of Navajo weaving, but aesthetically and culturally it is not unlike the nineteenth-century blankets.

In plate 1 the static dimension is most predominantly expressed by the dark blue (nearly black) center. This dark color is not to be associated with the Navajo blue (*dootł'izh*) which is typified by the blue of the daytime sky and the green of growing vegetation. Instead, this dark blue is more likely to be associated by the Navajo with the darkness of night, a static time and color. The static center contrasts with the active areas on each end of the shawl. The activity on the ends is expressed both by the active color red, associated with the female and with fertility (Witherspoon, 1975a:17–18), and by the diamonds which move in linear, horizontal, and parallel directions. If read vertically, the pattern moves from the active bottom end to the static center and on to the active top. However, since the static center is proportionally double the size of either active end, the pattern may be read in the active-static-static-active sequence. This sequence, as noted above, is associated with activity and creativity, as well as protection from evil. Black is worn as protection from evil and danger.

Blankets were worn by Navajos for warmth, for aesthetic expression, and for power and protection. Kahlenberg and Berlant comment that: "The blankets of the Navajos thus possessed a force beyond that customary for a single piece of apparel." They add that to a Navajo his blanket was like a "second skin" (1972:15). It is likely that this particular shawl or blanket (pl. 1) gave its owner or wearer a particular sense of protection from danger, and probably was worn by the patient of a blackening rite, both during and after the ceremony.

The active/static dimensions of this blanket are also expressed in the active color red enclosed by the static rectangles which are static both in color and shape, but which are uniquely arranged in an active shape (diamond). This active area created by the flowing diamonds is set off by the thin dark lines which provide a transitional space between the static center and the extremely active diamonds at the ends.

The balance here between the static center and the active ends seems to express the cultural emphasis on restrained aggressiveness, controlled movement and activity, and refined adaptability. It also seems relevant that activity here proceeds from a static center, as in the case where thought, the static inner form, proceeds to speech, the active outer form. The symmetry of this blanket also reflects the cultural emphasis on balance, order, and harmony.

The blanket in plate 2 expresses an emphasis on motion and activity, with the static dimension clearly put in a subordinate, interior position. The motion is linear and continuative, read either horizontally in the active and static spaces expressed by the yellow ochre and dark (green) colors set off and apart by the white and dark lines, or vertically in the active unidirectional arrows in the center and the active bidirectional entities on each side of the center. The bidirectional entities on the sides have a center that is static in shape and color, with active appendages. This then is contrasted by an active color arranged in a static (rectangular) shape. The static rectangle is enclosed in a static color (white) but this static color is in an active shape, with active appendages. These directional entities are then enclosed in a dark, static space which is set off on both sides by the active space composed of yellow ochre. The result is a careful, intricate, and delicate handling of static and active shapes, colors, and spaces, all arranged in a series alternating between static and active dimensions. The overall emphasis is on activity and movement, dynamic beauty and harmony.

The blanket in plate 3 possesses an active center space bordered on each side by static spaces created by stripes of white and dark blue. These static spaces then are bordered by active spaces, created by the diagonal lines and small angularly shaped entities on each side of them. Aesthetically this blanket illustrates a very sophisticated use of color. Contrasting and complementary colors are used to create visual brilliance and plastic space. This use of visual brilliance and plastic space anticipates the emphasis upon and use of color in contemporary color field painting.

The blanket in plate 4 illustrates the Navajo concept of movement from the center outward. Sandpaintings are made from the center outward. The movement from the center outward is complemented by the circular movement of the color arrangement. Black (static) space is in the center, bordered on both sides by two active colors, and then black is repeated again. Thus the arrangement of colored space follows the pattern static-active-active-static. Aesthetically, this blanket is dazzling but to me it is not as pleasing and sophisticated as the one in plate 3.

In plate 5 very active and contrasting designs are superimposed onto a static background. Previously I have referred to red as an active color. It can also be a static color and can be substituted for black (cf. p. 145). Red is not one of the four cardinal colors of the Navajo, and that allows it to be more easily interchanged. The design here is very intricate and complex. Repetition of contrast in color, line, and direction is the pictorial emphasis of this blanket. There is a contrast of value in the extensive use of black and white in close opposition to each other. There is a directional contrast where linear designs oppose each other diagonally. There is also a contrast between vertical and diagonal lines. The extensive repetition of these contrasts in every part and aspect of the design gives the blanket a visually energized surface.

Plate 6 is a modern example of weaving done in the Crystal area of the reservation. It utilizes a larger number of colors and beautifully contrasts fine discriminations of active and brilliant colors with darker and grayish tones. The result is an energized surface with alternating static and active spaces. The use of color in this rug anticipates principles and patterns found in contemporary color field painting. Particularly this rug parallels some of the work of Gene Davis whose huge multicolored paintings are based on striped motifs. His "cool buzz saw" painting is comparable to this rug because it contrasts brilliant colors with darker and grayer colors.

Navajo cultural categories are extensively reflected in plate 6, especially the cardinal number of four. The striped motif accentuates the four active spaces based on arrow-like designs and movements. Each of these arrow-like designs has four arrows, which alternate in the direction of their pointing between "in" and "out." From a center space, the arrows in both directions point out, then in, and then out again. The arrows on each edge end with half of the third arrow shown. From several perspectives there are three sets of "in" and "out" pointing arrows, but in each case the third is incomplete. Culturally three symbolizes incompletion, whereas four symbolizes completion. The artist here is thus creating an image in which the accentuated activity of the four active spaces extends beyond the surface of the rug. This feature is also characteristic of paintings done by Jackson Pollock.

As a general appraisal of Navajo woven blankets, Anthony Berlant, well-known artist and sculptor, and Mary Kahlenberg, curator of textiles and costumes at the Los Angeles County Museum, offer the following:

The visual impact of their blankets conveys the strength of Navajo culture and tradition. . . .

In visual power and force of statement Navajo blankets represent a high point in the history of American Indian art. The expressive use of color and energy controlled on a two-dimensional surface is remarkable, especially if we consider the great number of fine individual examples that can be found. The general level of quality was very high both in terms of weaving technique and visual expression (1972:42, 70).

Navajo sandpainting is a male-linked art form that accompanies most major Navajo ceremonials. The designs are established parts of the ritual and must not be significantly altered if the ritual is to be effective. These designs are made on the earthen floor of the hogan. The surface upon which the painting is made is cleaned and smoothed. The designs vary from a few inches to more than twenty feet in diameter, with most paintings averaging from three to six feet in diameter. The painting is done by letting dry pigments trickle through the thumb and flexed index finger. The dry pigments are made primarily from red, yellow, and white sandstone and various mixtures of these colors, but pigments made from colored corn meal, plant pollens, crushed flower petals, and charcoal are also used.

The sandpaintings are made by several men under the direction of the chanter or medicine man. Just as Reichard learned to weave, on many occasions I have enjoyed the opportunity to help create a sandpainting.

The sandpaintings depict the *Diyin Dine'é* and other sacred entities. They recall significant episodes of mythical drama. The mythical dramas revolve around a cultural hero's unfortunate plight and diseased condition, and his or her ultimate cure through identification with, and sometimes compulsive control of, a deity or deities. The disease is caused by some sort of disruption in the proper and normal order of things and is cured by a restoration of the proper order. The patient in his or her plight is identified with the cultural hero who contracted a similar disease or plight in the same way the patient did. In the curing ritual the patient follows in the footsteps of the hero of the myth, sings the songs he or she sang, prays the prayers he or she prayed, and ultimately acquires and exerts the power to restore health and order to his or her self and world that the hero acquired and exerted.

The myth, retold in the songs and prayers of the ritual, places the patient's illness in a cultural context where it can be understood and eventually cured. From the myth the patient learns that his or her plight and illness is not new, and that both its cause and treatment are known. To be cured, all the patient has to do is to repeat what has been done before. It has to be done sincerely, however, and this sincerity is expressed in concentration and dedication. The sandpainting depicts the desired order of things, and places the patient in this beautiful and ordered world. The patient thus becomes completely identified with the powerful and curing agents of the universe. The patient undresses to the extent modesty permits (men to a G-string and women to a skirt) and sits on the painting. Where appropriate and possible the patient's body parts—feet, knees, legs, etc.—are placed on the corresponding body parts of the deity with whom the patient is identified. In addition, the medicine man applies sand from the body parts of the depicted deity to corresponding body parts of the patient's body. Spectators and family members may also apply the sand to corresponding parts of their bodies as well. This is done for sanctification, blessing, and protection.

After the sandpainting has fulfilled its aesthetic and ritual purpose, the sand is carefully collected and deposited at some out-of-the-way place to the north. The symbolic representation of various sacred beings and things is considered to be effective in attracting them to the ceremonial hogan and thus enabling the patient to absorb their curative power.

Notwithstanding the important ritual functions of the sandpaintings, they also have great aesthetic appeal to Navajos. The painters take a special interest and pride in the quality of their work, and many men travel from ceremony to ceremony mainly to participate in the art forms—singing, poetry, drama, and painting—of the ritual. The ceremonies are really a symphony of the arts and they have great aesthetic appeal to Navajo participants and spectators. Where else can one go to and participate in a symphony of the arts while simultaneously being physically, morally, and intellectually sanctified and blessed?

The aesthetic appeal of the forms and designs of sandpaintings is also demonstrated in their extensive use in other Navajo art forms. This is particularly true in weaving where many designs and forms are taken from sandpaintings. These designs, however, also appear in Navajo silver work and in the oil paintings and drawings of contemporary Navajo artists. Such replications of these sacred designs and forms are potentially dangerous to their creators, and many purists among the Navajos deplore this secularization and profanation of sacred forms and symbols. Nevertheless, the aesthetic appeal of these designs and forms seems to have, in many cases, overriden the fear of the dangers inherent in the secular use of sacred forms. As elsewhere in Navajo culture, movement, repetition, balance and harmony, and controlled or restrained emotion and force are dominant themes in Navajo sandpaintings.

There have been two studies of Navajo art and culture. One was done in the 1950s by George Mills and the other was done in the 1960s by Evelyn Payne Hatcher. Both studies involved very little fieldwork or firsthand acquaintance with Navajo language or culture. They were both done from a psychological—culture and personality—orientation, concentrating on personality traits reflected in the art forms. Despite these major handicaps, both works offer some perceptive and relevant conclusions with regard to Navajo sandpaintings in particular (since this was the focus of both works, Hatcher to an even greater extent than Mills).

Hatcher found movement to be a major theme of Navajo sandpainting:

Movement as perceived by the Navajo in drypainting seems to rest largely on dynamic repetition or rotational symmetry, and on assigned sequences of color. . . . I view the movement in drypaintings, especially the circular ones, in terms of rotational motion, and consider the outward "movement" of structural lines in terms of tension or vitality. To me the radiating lines definitely move outward rather than converge, and are often opposed and contained by the border (1974:170–71).

Mills came to a similar conclusion about the portrayal of movement in sandpaintings:

One more major notion is striking in this art, which, according to definition, seems so stereotyped, and that is, that the paintings are generally not static. The literary convention prescribes motion and the pictorial devices carry it out. People "follow one another" or "face," animals seem to move, indeed whole compositions . . . actually circulate in the space they occupy (1959:491).

Reichard also found a symbolic representation of movement in her analysis: "an unpublished painting in the Huckel Collection, *Buffalo People at the Mountain-of-motion*, represents not the mountains, rocks, clouds, and waters but their motion, their life, expressed by color associated with light . . . " (1950a:252).

The movement, activity, and vitality of Navajo sandpaintings is, however, always held under control. Mills concludes his analysis of movement and spacing with this evaluation: "I judge that Navajos enjoy a healthy balance of dynamism and control, that their vitality is unimpaired, and that they recognize and adjust to external conditions" (1959:40).

Movement under control in Navajo sandpainting provides the basis for the balance, harmony, and order that are expressed in these works of art. This is especially expressed in the dynamic symmetry of Navajo sandpaintings. Mills notes that "balance and symmetry also relate to Navajo concern [with] order. In Parker's terms, symmetry flatters their craving for unity; it provides an agreeable feeling of steadfastness and stability" (1959:146). Hatcher added:

> Just as symmetry does not employ the opposition of the bilateral form, so the movement which is conveyed by the figures is not that of opposed or conflicting actions. The anthropomorphic figures are not in violent action. The movement is a collective one. All move in the same direction at the same rate like celestial bodies. This is very striking when one comes to consider the myths which the paintings illustrate. Illustrations in the European tradition would center on the battles of Monster Slayer with much use of conflicting movement in the form of opposed diagonals and active lines full of wiggly curves, such as can be seen in the numerous representations of St. George and the Dragon. But the drypaintings, both in content and in form, glorify not the conflict but the order achieved as a result of it (1974:171).

Both Mills and Hatcher found that Navajo art reflected strong and rich emotions. Mills commented that "there is agreement that movement manifests richness of inner life. 'The urge to represent objects in motion or in action seems . . . to be an indication of a vividly imaginative and vitally strong, often creative personality' (Kinget, 1952:111)" (1959:136). Mills adds that although the Navajo appear to be strongly emotional, their art work illustrates a tendency to turn their emotions inward (1959:132).

Plate 7, showing the whirling logs sandpainting found in the Night and Feather chants, clearly illustrates a circular, spinning motion around a set, static hub which is colored black, a static color. This seems to reflect appropriately the idea that the inner form of things is static and the outer form of things is active, and that activity proceeds from and around a static interior. Attached to the central hub by white (static) lines are four sacred plants:

beans, corn, squash, and tobacco. The plants are painted in the active blue colors. Holy People, or *Yee'íí*, also move in a sunwise direction around the central hub.

Aesthetically, this painting illustrates both an energized and a transparent surface. The painting also expresses the Navajo concept and pattern of contained force. The spiraling movement of the figures is contained both by their attachment to and relationship with the central hub and by the outlying *Yee'íí* figure which nearly encircles their fully energized pattern. The energized surface is also enhanced by the extensive use of color contrasts against a neutral background. The moving figures and extensive color contrasts in them balance with the rather extensive neutral background. Thus the visual weight of this painting is light and transparent, rather than heavy and opaque.

This painting also illustrates dynamic symmetry as opposed to static symmetry. Static symmetry is absolute balance without any oppositions, contrasts, or disequilibrium. Dynamic symmetry expresses motion and energy created by oppositions, contrasts, and disequilibrium. Here contrasts are found in diagonal lines and figures contrasted to vertical and horizontal lines and figures, in the use of pure colors against a neutral background, and in the alternation of colors in opposing figures.

Silversmithing is an art form of both men and women. Most silversmiths are men but there is no ideological or prescriptive basis for the predominance of male silversmiths. The explanation probably lies in the fact that in weaving women have a free design art form, whereas sandpainting allows only a very limited opportunity to express one's individuality and creativity. Silversmithing thus offers this added opportunity for creativity to male artists; however, some Navajo women are also excellent silversmiths.

Plate 8 shows an example of Navajo silver work. Again it represents movement going outward from a static center or hub. The uneven number of leaves (three) is active as opposed to even numbers which are normally static. The curved lines and leaves moving outward from the center to the corners also express energy and activity. The many repetitions of curvilinear

PLATE 1. WOVEN WOMAN'S SHAWL

Courtesy of Museum of the American Indian, Heye Foundation

PLATE 2. WOVEN WOOL BLANKET A

Courtesy of Museum of the American Indian, Heye Foundation

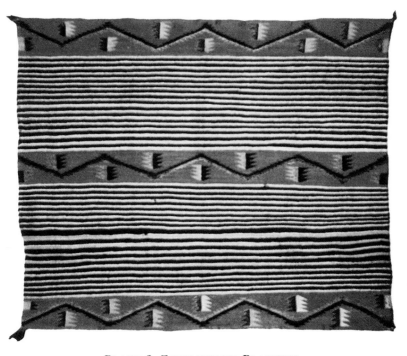

PLATE 3. ZONE-WOVEN BLANKET

Courtesy of Museum of the American Indian, Heye Foundation

PLATE 4. SADDLE BLANKET

Courtesy of Museum of the American Indian, Heye Foundation

PLATE 5. WOVEN WOOL BLANKET B
Courtesy of Museum of the American Indian, Heye Foundation

PLATE 6. CRYSTAL RUG BY SARAH WILLIAMS OF
COAL MINE MESA, ARIZONA
Courtesy of Read Mullan Collection, Heard Museum, Phoenix, Arizona

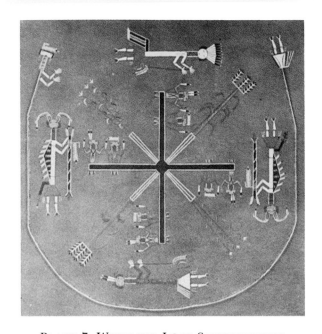

PLATE 7. WHIRLING LOGS SANDPAINTING

Reprinted, by permission, from Southwestern Indian Ceremonials, *by Tom Bahti,*
© *1970 KC Publications*

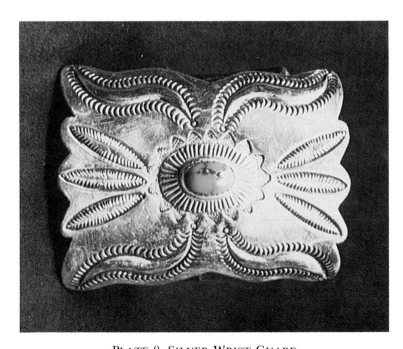

PLATE 8. SILVER WRIST GUARD

Courtesy of Museum of the American Indian, Heye Foundation

lines and shapes give the piece dynamic movement which both flows outward and around and is harmonious and balanced. The short, straight lines superimposed on the curvilinear borders of the various figures give the piece contrasts in direction, activity, and texture.

Other Navajo art forms include pottery, moccasins, leather work, basketry, and watercolor and oil painting. Although there is not sufficient space here to discuss each of these art forms separately, they are mentioned to demonstrate how thoroughly integrated art is in Navajo culture. Many Navajos have gained national reputations as outstanding artists; however, most Navajo artists prefer to create beauty on a daily basis in common endeavors. Enjoying the opportunity to create beauty in their minds and project it onto reality, they sell their works of art anonymously. Their inner satisfaction as an artist does not derive from public display or public acclaim but from private creation and renewal.

Just as Navajo concepts of thought and speech, mind and matter, were contrasted to empiricism and positivism, and just as the Navajo philosophy of language was compared with other views and philosophies of language, I will now attempt to place Navajo art in context with and in contrast to art traditions in the West. In terms of the major art traditions or modes of the West—classicism, romanticism, and realism—Navajo art represents a delicate and unique combination of aspects of classicism and romanticism. Navajo artists show little inclination toward renaissance-type realism, which emphasized the creation of pictorial space through linear perspective. Navajo art seems to be able to combine the emphasis on order and balance found in classicism with the forcefulness, energy, and expressiveness found in romanticism. Kahlenberg and Berlant express this succinctly in their aesthetic appraisal of nineteenth-century Navajo blankets:

The breadth and space these blankets contain and the uncanny blend of absolute calm with consistent, balanced energy mark them as a high point in the Navajo weaving tradition. . . .

Early first phase chief pattern blankets reveal the essence of
Navajo aesthetics with its paradoxical harmony and aggressiveness. . . .

They have a force and color energy that is full and exuber-
ant but always under control (1972:16–17).

Navajo art has had a subtle, little-known relationship with and
impact upon contemporary art. This is illustrated by the exhibition of Navajo blankets put together by Kahlenberg and Berlant.
This exhibition, which started at the Los Angeles County Museum
and then toured nationally, and which was put together from the
personal collections of many important contemporary artists such
as Arman, Benghis, Caro, Dine, Francis, Hockney, Johns, Allen
Jones, Judd, Lindner, Marden, McCracken, Morris, Ed Moses,
Kenneth Noland, Ken Price, Tony Smith, Stella, Warhol, and
Zox, brought the visual vitality of Navajo art to a greater degree
of public awareness. It seems clear, however, that many contemporary artists were already aware of this visual vitality of Navajo
art and had been inspired by it. Recent developments in the
thinking and perception of contemporary artists have run parallel
with many aspects of Navajo aestheticism. Berlant and Kahlenberg claim that "contemporary artists have led us to a new way of
seeing these blankets, one which would not have been readily
accessible 30 years ago" (1972:71).

Jackson Pollock, the revolutionary American painter whose impact upon twentieth-century art is probably only surpassed by
Picasso, was possibly the first, and certainly the most famous,
modern artist to be inspired by Navajo art. Picasso, inspired by
African art, developed cubism, while Pollock, inspired by Navajo
sandpainting, rejected cubism and developed action and field
painting. Alberto Busignani notes that "Jackson Pollock released
art in the United States from its long European bondage"
(1971:cover flap).

Pollock's early and formative work is summarized by Bryan Robertson (1970):

The drawings and studies relating to the period c. 1930–34 are most revealing: all the seeds are contained in them for Pollock's future development. They embody in the simplest terms his essential characteristics as an artist. The first impression is of an almost incessant preoccupation with movement. . . .

Even in these early studies, Pollock is trying to get through and beyond the restrictions of physical reality and to capture and transmit a distillation of energy, drawn out of the flux of human experience and thrown back again into the flux of time (Quoted in Busignani, 1971:12).

Pollock rejected technological society and the exploitation of human beings in consumption-oriented cultures. He claimed that the orientation toward production and consumption of things reduced man and the natural environment to episodes of the productive machine. Busignani shows that Pollock's rejection of a cultural tradition he did not feel was his own "was accompanied by his acceptance of another kind of history, intimately linked to nature, magic, symbols, etc. . . . Pollock found it recorded in the practices of the American Indians, especially in the sand paintings of the Navaho" (1971:21).

Pollock was born in Wyoming and in his youth traveled extensively in the Southwest. Even after he eventually settled in New York and became famous, he continued periodic trips to the Southwest and paid close attention to Navajo works of art. Pollock once explained:

My painting does not come from the easel. I hardly ever stretch my canvas before painting. I prefer to tack the unstretched canvas to the hard wall or floor. I need the resistance of a hard surface. On the floor I am at ease. I feel nearer, more a part of the painting, since this way I can walk around it, work from the four sides and literally be "in" the painting. This is akin to the method of the Indian sand painters of the West (Quoted in Busignani, 1971:22).

Robertson, an art historian, observes that out of all of Pollock's experiences,

... he was most directly affected by the practice of Indian sandpainting.

The form of art is part of a ritual. Its conception is opposed to the modern European idea of art as a separate activity for its own sake, with no magical properties and with no part to play in a ritual. European art is permanent: we conserve it and restore it, we guard it in museums, and we buy and sell it as a commodity. The idea of a temporary art made only to serve a ritual mythology and placed at the mercy of the elements is strange to us. The idea was not strange to Pollock, and his sympathy for it provides us with the crux of his personality as an artist and the most radical clue towards an understanding of his pictorial inclinations (Quoted in Busignani, 1971:22).

Pollock's pictorial effort was to unify the picture by unifying experience and by seeing all things in the universe as part of a vast general order. He sought to avoid fragmentation for its own sake or for the sake of decoration (Busignani, 1971:14, 33). Busignani adds:

How clearly Pollock recognized his own attitude may be seen by his own emphasis on Navajo painting. . . . The coincidence between representation and action or even the annihilation of representation in action, constituted the ultimate act, the final truth of a conception of existence which brought together history and nature, past, present and future in the act of creation. The 19th century image of the romantic poet who himself assumes an ethical as well as an aesthetic responsibility is defined in this henceforth absolute identification of being with doing and of doing with creating. The only morality, and therefore the only truth, lies in becoming totally intermingled with one's creation, making painting and the act of painting a constant intervention into reality (1971:38).

Like Navajo artists, Pollock tried to express forcefulness, energy, and motion without the loss of order, balance, and control. Like nineteenth-century Navajo blankets and Navajo sandpaintings, Pollock's expression of movement seems to extend beyond the edges of the canvas. Pollock's work, and thus Navajo art as well, was germinal to the development of the currently emphasized color field painting.

Three important features that are common to both Navajo art and color field painting are linearity, lightness, and openness. Linearity is expressed in a unity and balance of pattern and in repetition. Lightness is found in the delicate balance of figure-ground relationships. Openness is expressed in transparency, as opposed to opacity. Navajo sandpaintings are very transparent. One can see through the surface figures to the background upon which they are placed, yet both are perceived as a unified representation. Contemporary artists doing color field painting are now trying to achieve this same quality. An energized surface is also common both to contemporary color field painting and to Navajo works of art.

A final parallel between traditional Navajo art and modern art in the West is abstract expressionism. Kahlenberg and Berlant comment on this:

The premises of "abstract art" are no longer controversial, but neither are they rooted in our society. Abstraction was not a special "artist's" vocabulary for the Navajo who wove these blankets; rather, it was a means for personal expression within their society. The Navajo weaver dealt with many of the same concerns as do contemporary artists, but in the more integral Navajo culture these concerns were central and shared by everyone (1972:71).

Navajo art thus expresses Navajo experiences, and Navajo experiences are mediated by the concepts of and orientations to the world found in Navajo language and culture. All experiences are directed toward the ideals of *hózhǫ́*, and *hózhǫ́* is the intellectual, moral, biological, emotional, and aesthetic experience of beauty. A Navajo experiences beauty most poignantly in creating it and in expressing it, not in observing it or preserving it. The experience of beauty is dynamic; it flows to one and from one; it is found not in things, but in relationships among things. Beauty is not to be preserved but to be continually renewed in oneself and expressed in one's daily life and activities. To contribute to and be a part of this universal *hózhǫ́* is both man's special blessing and his ultimate destiny.

Conclusion

In the Introduction, culture was defined as a set of conceptions of and orientations to reality embodied in and expressed by symbols and symbolic forms (cf. p. 3). It was also claimed that it is from a people's conception of the nature of reality, its operation and constitution, and their relationship to it, that emanate a set of value orientations, behavioral codes, and classificatory structures. In previous chapters the Navajo conception of reality, its constitution and operation, have been discussed. It was found that the primary metaphysical assumption on which the Navajo view of the world is built is the opposition between active and static phenomena or active and static phases of phenomena. In chapter 1 it was shown how this dualism constitutes the metaphysical foundation and ideological framework for Navajo ideas concerning the nature of thought and speech, knowledge and language, and word and element. Chapter 2 illustrated how these conceptions of reality provide the ideological concepts behind the Navajo doctrine of the compulsive power of language and ritual. Chapter 3 discussed how the dualism of active and static forms the primary contrast from which various complex classificatory schemes are ultimately derived. Chapter 4 showed how this dualism is also reflected in Navajo art. Here I want to discuss how these concepts of reality are translated into everyday behavioral patterns and value orientations.

In recent years it has become analytically useful to distinguish ethos from world view. A people's world view constitutes a basically intellectual view of reality, whereas a people's ethos expresses the behavioral themes and value orientations that are implicit in and derived from the world view. Given their view of the world as expressed in the symbols of language, color, art, and ritual, Navajos find their way of life not only to be an appropriate adaptation to the world as it is portrayed in the world view but also to be

179

absolutely necessary to survival. A Navajo not only feels he should follow certain observances and avoid others; he finds it dangerous to do otherwise. A Navajo does not say a prayer to the inner form of a deer explaining his need for the deer and asking for the deer's indulgence simply because it is a kind and gracious thing to do; he does so also because it reminds him of the deer's right to life and the necessity for him not to be excessive or overindulgent in his use of the deer, for such excessive behavior could throw the whole world out of harmony and balance and that would be dangerous to his own survival.

Associated with the Navajo concepts of static and active are an emphasis upon motion and a concern to keep it under control. In accordance with the premises that motion is inherent in air and that beings which inhale and exhale air manifest the greatest capacity for movement, Navajos have posited the existence of instanding air souls which control the movements of the bodies they occupy. The most highly refined of these movements is speech, and beings which can speak a language are considered to have greater capacity to control movement than those which can only cry or call. Speech is a highly refined use of air and a very sophisticated form of movement; accordingly, an equally sophisticated inner form—thought—is appropriately paired with it.

Thought is of primary importance in the Navajo world, for it is not only the source of control but the means by which the goal of control may be attained. The goal of control is the creation of form, order, harmony, balance, and beauty. In order for people to produce hózhǫ́ in their world, they must be able first to create hózhǫ́ in their minds. Everything in the universe cannot be materially constituted or reordered in the mind, but mental ordering and reordering of the universe can take place through symbols. Symbols come in both linguistic and nonlinguistic forms, for in ritual both language and art are utilized in efforts to reorder the universe and restore it to the condition of hózhǫ́.

Symbols antedate the existence of people and are a prerequisite to the creation of form and beauty in the world. Symbols are primordial, for in the beginning were the word and the element, the symbol and the symbolized. Symbol is dependent on element, knowledge is dependent on symbol, thought is dependent on knowledge, creation and control are dependent on thought, but motion is not dependent on man's control. Motion is inherent in air, and because air permeates the universe and gives it life and motion, motion is primordial and occurs both in conditions controlled by man and in those out of his control. All motion, conditions, and events, however, can be controlled and compelled by man through ritual action, given adequate knowledge and proper performance.

From the concepts outlined above, four principal value orientations or emphases may be delineated: (1) emphasis on activity and creativity; (2) emphasis on control; (3) emphasis on balance and order; and (4) emphasis on beauty and harmony. Below I will discuss how each of these value orientations or emphases finds expression in the everyday life and behavior of Navajos.

EMPHASIS ON ACTIVITY AND CREATIVITY

Creativity implies activity and transformation. A creative person is an active and dynamic person, believing that the world can be transformed into more attractive and expressive forms. Creation is positive and expressive action, and action is the essence of life. Navajos cherish life and place a high value on creativity, the highest and most positive expression of life.

As activity is the foundation of creativity and the positive expression of life, Navajos value and encourage energy in their everyday life. One of the most highly cherished attributes or traits a Navajo may have is *biinéí* 'he is very energetic, full of life and activity'. A person who is *biinéí* never lets the sun rise before he does and always runs to the east to greet the rising sun. One who eagerly and energetically gathers and chops the firewood and carries the water is described by the term *biinéí*. An industrious woman who gets up early to cook the food, arrange the household, do the weaving, and care for the children and the sheep is also referred to by the term *biinéí*. People who have this quality are said not only to live a long life but to make life possible for others. *Biinéí* expresses the Navajo concept of physical conditioning, and is derived from a positive mental attitude toward life and activity.

In Navajo mythology the emphasis upon activity and creativity seems to be expressed by the recurrent theme of the traveling cultural hero who adds to the knowledge and life of the people through his creative experiences while traveling. In fact, Navajo mythology seems to sanctify travel and motion:

> When Bitahatini, the hero of the myth of the Night Chant, finally stands face to face with the goal of all goals, he feels fear rise in his heart, but his supernatural companion encourages him, saying: "Fear not. Your body is holy. You are holy as you travel" (Matthews, 1902:184; quoted in Astrov, 1950:49).

In mythology it is the traveler who seeks out and finds the gods. It is the traveler who, through misfortune or misadventure, discovers new knowledge. It is the traveler who as a novice acquires power and immunity through contact with the gods and their symbols and charms. And it is the traveling cultural hero who in pain and illness finds the cherished herb that can diffuse pain and restore health.

The emphasis on creativity has led Navajos to accept, adopt, and adapt many things and practices from other peoples. Many aspects of Navajo culture have been adopted from other cultures and incorporated into Navajo life. This has been done creatively, so that the essence and core of Navajo life and culture have not been disrupted or destroyed but have been enhanced. Many writers and historians have commented on the ability of the Navajo to absorb without being absorbed. This ability is derived from a capacity to make creative syntheses.

It is the creative nature of the Navajos that allows them to survive and even prosper in the most difficult and dire circumstances. Twice in their recent history they have endured and risen from traumatic experiences of poverty and subjugation. One of these was when Kit Carson and the cavalry destroyed their sheep, corn fields, and fruit trees, and thus forced them to surrender. Then they were marched on the "Long Walk" to Fort Sumner where they were held in captivity for four years. The plan was to hold them there indefinitely or until they became civilized city-dwellers and farmers. Instead their creativity enabled them to persuade the government to allow them to return to their home-land. When they returned, they had nothing. Their property had all been destroyed, lost, or confiscated. The government issued them less than one sheep per person, a few horses, and some plows, and told them to survive on their own. They not only survived but they prospered. In less than fifty years their livestock holdings increased nearly a hundredfold. Then in the 1930s the government again destroyed most of their livestock, dissolved their tribal government, and arrested and jailed most of their leaders who rejected this disastrous action. Again, however, they survived this traumatic period and since then have been doing rather well under difficult conditions.

This ability not only to make do but even to do well with a dearth of things and opportunities is also manifested in their daily lives. Navajos have an almost uncanny ability to improvise solutions to apparently insoluble problems. This includes repairing cars and trucks without parts or tools, often by using wire, inner tubes, rope or even rocks, sticks, and bones. It also includes getting cars out of mud, snow, and sand when they appear to be hopelessly stuck. It also manifests itself in their ability to grow corn in the desert. Their positive thinking is demonstrated when they plant corn in dry soil that has not felt rain 'for months.

Reichard observed many of these same traits and characteristics:

One day at the well I neglected to tie a knot properly and our only good bucket fell to the bottom. Marie laughed and sent a child to a house in sight for a long hooked wire. After

Marie had fished up the bucket and we had finished our work, the car was caught in dry quicksands. With the aid of some men who came to the well we worked for three hours before we got out. But at no time was there a dearth of ideas as to *how* to work (1968:198).

This ability to create with little or nothing is probably best seen in Navajo art work. The Navajos have no brushes, no canvas, no paint, and no formal instruction, yet they have made paintings that have aroused the respect and admiration of many outstanding contemporary artists, including the greatest American painter of this century, Pollock, who has incorporated elements of Navajo artistry in his own works. They find their "paints" in colored corn meal, plant pollen, crushed flower petals, charcoal, and in yellow, red, white, and charcoal sandstone. They mix charcoal and white sand to get gray, charcoal and red sand to get brown, and red and white sand to get pink. Instead of brushes, they use their hands, carefully letting the colored sand trickle between the thumb and index finger. With nothing more than a few logs and sticks, a little rope, skillful hands, and a creative mind, they transform wool from the backs of sheep into beautifully woven rugs with complex and intricate designs.

Another dimension of Navajo daily life which reveals the emphasis on creativity is the prevalence of humor in their activities and conversations. Humor lubricates the rhythms of life and transforms difficult and frustrating situations into bearable and even pleasant ones. Navajo humor emphasizes wit and is often very subtle. At the basis of this humor are creative thought and creative expression. A Navajo who can "see" and express the humor of situations is highly cherished and appreciated as a family member, a guest, a visitor, or a fellow worker.

Navajo joke tellers are really story tellers and dramatists. The humorous stories strikingly parallel, at least in their basic plot, Navajo myths. They are all about a central character who meets misfortune, illness, or injury by making a fool out of himself or herself. Their foolish behavior which results in misfortune is clearly due to ignorance, inadvertence, or carelessness. If there is a subtle moral message in these humorous stories, it is one that says that if a person is to avoid misfortune and danger he must seek knowledge, wisdom, and maturity and must be careful and deliberate in his behavior.

The tremendous emphasis and value Navajos place on humor is reflected in the First Laugh rite. The first time a child laughs out is a time for honor and celebration. The child through its parents calls a party in which the child's first laugh is celebrated by the child giving salt and bread to all participants. Without such a party or rite, Navajos say the child will lose its sense of humor and become stingy. In the Navajo metaphor, humor and generosity are closely linked traits. They are both social acts that lubricate social interaction and enhance social harmony.

Navajos are an active, dynamic, and creative people. Their culture emphasizes the power of the mind to think and to create, and this impulse to create finds expression in the many symbolic creations of Navajo language, art, and ritual. It is also revealed in the way they daily improvise solutions to apparently insoluble problems, in the way they synthesize the apparently irreconcilable, in the way they translate simple and common things into beautiful forms and patterns, and in the way they ritually transform unpleasant and seemingly unbearable conditions into bearable and blessed ones.

EMPHASIS ON CONTROL

The world of the Navajo is characterized by movements in space and transformations in states of being through time. None of these movements or transformations are inherently good or evil, but are potentially both good and evil. That which distinguishes the good from the evil is control. All powers of motion and transformation can be used for the good of man if they can be controlled by man. All things and beings and their respective powers that are outside of man's control are dangerous and potentially evil. For the Navajo, evil (*hóchxǫ'*) is not negative in a moral or ethical sense but negative in a pragmatic or realistic sense. Evil is misfortune, illness, premature death, drought, famine, or some other such tragedy, all of which may be caused by things and beings out of control.

For their safety, health, and well-being, the Navajos are interested in controlling both themselves and their environment. Their control of themselves involves the controlling of both their emotions and their behavior. Navajos avoid excess both in the expression of emotion and in the performance of duty. Excess is avoided primarily because of the lack of control it implies or suggests. Reichard notes that:

> Excess of any kind, of industrial pursuit, of religious ardor, of grief, of sexual intercourse, is deplored. It may bring on illness, bewilderment, weakness, and must be exorcised by a religious performance, the "Excess Chant." Once this phase of the subject is understood, it is obvious that Navajo literature would hardly develop along the lines of the French literature in which the definition of passion is a major theme. (1950b:197)

Navajos attempt to keep their emotions under control and seldom verbalize intense emotions of either love or hate, kindness or anger. Navajo emotional life proceeds in a low key and at a slow pace. Even the tremendous emphasis on humor leads only to restrained, never boisterous, laughter. This emphasis on moderation is also exhibited in Navajo speech patterns which are not characterized by the superlatives to which many Americans are accustomed.

When the enclitic *-goo* 'in this manner or direction' is suffixed to the term *hózhǫ́*, the semantic result is an admonition to be careful and deliberate. Although Navajos value activity and energy, they are deliberate in their actions and cautious in their use of energy, always keeping their actions and emotions under control. Many times when I have shown movies taken among the Navajo to non-Navajos, I have been asked whether the movies were taken in slow motion or why I was showing them in slow motion. In track events Navajo youth never seem to excell in the high-speed sprints, but often do rather well in the long distance runs.

The Navajo style of slow, careful, and deliberate behavior, coupled with the lack of passion and superlatives in speech, does not lend itself well to getting ahead in the modern, high-speed and high-strung society where excessive sensuality and superlative expressiveness are commonplace, but it also does not lead to heart disease and ulcers. Very few Navajos have died of a heart attack, and ulcers were unknown in traditional Navajo society. Traditionally a very high percentage of Navajos who survived childhood went on to live beyond eighty and even one hundred years of age.

When their world is disrupted by evil, disorder, and disharmony, Navajos attempt to restore good, order, and harmony to their environment through ritual control. Effective ritual control involves ritual knowledge, so ritual knowledge is highly valued and carefully and restrictively transmitted. Reichard notes the following:

> Knowledge is valued as training; it is not of itself emotional but its possession gives rise to some of the most marked emotional attitudes. The stem for 'know, possess knowledge, be acquainted with, be able to analyze, summarize' (-zįįł) is . . . closely related, phonetically and grammatically, as well as semantically to the stem 'be holy, blessed, sanctified' (yįįł) (1949:71–72).

Navajos believe that by careful and deliberate attention to oneself and to one's environment, accidents and misfortune can be avoided. By exercising the powers of his mind and by utilizing ritual knowledge a Navajo believes he can avoid tragedies, overcome evil, and insure a long and happy life. Reichard comments on this virtuosity of Navajo life:

> I have never ceased to wonder at the casualness with which life is carried on by the Navajo. The matter-of-factness with

which they meet emergencies stipulates not only great re-
sourcefulness but also perfect virtuosity, a control of the factors which go to make up different phases of life. Above all,
it involves a state of mind, which once attained is a comfortable possession (1968:195).

It is man's mind and his ability to create and use complex symbol
systems that puts him at the center of creation and gives him
the capacity and confidence to bless himself and beautify his
environment.

EMPHASIS ON BALANCE AND ORDER

The Navajo emphasis upon balance and order has been expressed
all through this book. Chapter 1 dealt with the Navajo interest in
and account of the origin of form and order; chapter 2 illustrated
how the moral order of the universe is restored when it has been
disrupted; chapter 3 revealed the extensive and intensive intellectual ordering or classifying of things in the Navajo universe;
chapter 4 showed how a concern for order and balance is reflected in Navajo works of art.

The emphasis on balance in the daily life of the Navajo is found
in their avoidance of excess in any area and in their pattern of
moderation in all things. The Navajo compulsion for order is
found in the numerous and frequent rites they perform and participate in to maintain and restore order. Their avoidance of
conflict and confrontation in interpersonal relations and their lack
of superlatives and extremism in conversation seem designed to
maintain and enhance social order.

Navajo intellectualism and aestheticism are balanced by a strong
orientation toward pragmatism and lightmindedness. Learning
for the sake of learning, art for the sake of art, work for the sake
of work have never made much sense to the Navajo. All these are
directed toward pragmatic ends. Of course, what is practical in
one set of cultural values is often ephemeral in another. To the

Navajo, the practical is that which contributes to order, harmon health, happiness, and beauty.

Their pragmatism is especially revealed in their attitude toward change. They have little or no sentimental reservations about changing aspects of their way of life when better ways of doing things are known and accessible. Not being fearful of alien ways nor being highly sentimental about their own, they readily explore and experiment with new ways of doing things. This applies to the areas of religion and art, as well as to patterns of subsistence and economics. Their interest in and experimentation with new ways of doing things does not, however, normally lead to change. Most often they soon resort to their own proven and established ways. They are not interested in change for the sake of change, only change for the sake of improvement and enhancement. Unlike Anglo-Americans they do not assume that the new is always or most likely better. In fact, if anything, they assume that the new, not having been proven by the test of time, will most likely prove to be not as good as that which they already have. Although not being fearful about change or not wishing to hold to tradition, Navajos are careful and deliberate about the changes they make in their way of life. When they do change, it does not usually involve the wholesale and unaltered adoption of alien ways, but a creative synthesis of alien ways with traditional modes.

Earlier I referred to the Navajo characteristic of lightmindedness, which I define as a lack of sentimentality, seriousness, and worry in their daily approach to life. Although highly reflective and philosophical, they do not dwell upon or worry about the "heavy" and the mentally burdensome things that cause Western intellectuals and reformers great anxiety. Although they think about such matters, they do not become overwhelmed by them. They accept the fact that there is much they do not know, and they try to make do as best they can with what they do know. A good example of this is their attitude toward life after death. Although there are some stories that people tell about the lingering existence of one's wind soul or ghost after the body is dead, and there is a more general and prevalent assumption that after death one's body and soul will be reincorporated into the universal state of *są'ah naagháii bik'eh hózhǫ*, most Navajos frankly admit that they do not know whether or not they will continue to exist in some fashion after death. They conclude that they will find out about that when they die. Until then, since there is no way of really knowing the answer to that, they figure they should not waste their lives in worrying about it. Instead they concentrate on that which they do have—this life—and all their efforts are directed toward making it happier, more harmonious, and more beautiful.

The Navajo approach to the death of a friend or kinsman is to mourn profusely for four days, then go through a rite of purification. The personal property of the deceased is buried with him or destroyed, and his name is never again mentioned for one year after his death. Even then the deceased's name is rarely mentioned. Their attitude toward the death of a loved one may be best summarized by the following quote:

One summer I left Ganado just before Red Point was to sing the Shooting Chant for a man who lived nearby. Several months later I received a letter from one of my interpreters in which he remarked in the characteristic Navajo way, "Red Point didn't sing the Shooting Chant after you left. The man died, that's the reason. We were all very sad about it, but as I told the family, 'We have plenty to do to take care of the living, we must not worry about the dead'" (Reichard, 1968:202).

In the Navajo emphasis upon mental power, mental creativity, and mental health, they see no place for worry or "heaviness." They do not become overly serious or concerned about matters beyond their control. Although they feel that they can control most things and they can resolve many of their problems, they also realize that sometimes things will get out of control or escape their control. What they can control, they try to control; what they cannot control, they accept without fretting or paranoia:

> When I first went to the Navajo country I used to worry, as do all new-comers, about this and that. I have now adopted the confidence the Navajo have in themselves which may perhaps be formulated, "If it is worth doing, we can do it, if it is not—and our inability to do it may prove it is not—what does it matter anyway?" (Reichard, 1968:195)

In the careful, deliberate, and orderly behavior of the Navajo, there is a delicate but definite balancing of pragmatism with idealism.

EMPHASIS ON BEAUTY AND HARMONY

If a Navajo is to be truly happy and healthy, beauty must dominate his thought and speech, and harmony must permeate his environment. Beauty flows from the mind or inner form of a person. Navajos have radiant personalities and the beauty they have within themselves seems to radiate from the inner core of their being. This can readily be seen in firsthand observation or even in photographs. When Old Man Buffalo Grass went to see Aileen O'Bryan at the Mesa Verde National Park so she could record much of what he knew about the history and beliefs of his people, he commented on the Navajo emphasis on beauty within: "You look at me and see only an ugly old man, but within I am filled with great beauty" (1956:vii).

Navajos generate hózhǫ in their minds and souls or incorporate hózhǫ within themselves by ritual identification with the Holy People who possess it. This ritual identification allows the hózhǫ that radiates from the Holy Person to extend to and be incorporated in the being and mind of the patient through prayer and song, symbol and sandpainting. The following song from the Blessingway rite (see also Wyman, 1970:233–34) illustrates this process:

Wherever I go *hózhǫ́* radiates before me.

Give me the feet of *Sǫ'ah Naagháii, of Bik'eh Hózhǫ́!*
Hózhǫ́ radiates before me.
As far as I gaze before me earth extends its *hózhǫ́,*
wherever I go *hózhǫ́* radiates behind me,
wherever I go *hózhǫ́* radiates behind me.

Give me the legs of *Sǫ'ah Naagháii, of Bik'eh Hózhǫ́!*
Hózhǫ́ radiates behind me.
As far as I gaze behind me earth usually extends its *hózhǫ́,*
wherever I go *hózhǫ́* radiates below me,
wherever I go *hózhǫ́* radiates below me.

Give me the body of *Sǫ'ah Naagháii, of Bik'eh Hózhǫ́!*
Hózhǫ́ radiates below me.
As far as I gaze below me, earth usually extends its *hózhǫ́,*
wherever I go *hózhǫ́* radiates above me,
wherever I go *hózhǫ́* radiates above me.

Give me the mind of *Sǫ'ah Naagháii, of Bik'eh Hózhǫ́!*
Hózhǫ́ radiates above me.
As far as I gaze above me earth usually extends its *hózhǫ́,*
wherever I go *hózhǫ́* radiates around me.
wherever I go *hózhǫ́* radiates around me.

Give me the speech of *Sǫ'ah Naagháii, of Bik'eh Hózhǫ́!*
Hózhǫ́ radiates around me.
As far as I gaze around me earth usually extends its *hózhǫ́,*
wherever I go *hózhǫ́* radiates around me,
wherever I go *hózhǫ́* radiates around me.

N. Scott Momaday, a Kiowa and Pulitzer Prize winning author, found that Navajos also perceive, enjoy, and relate to the beauty of the natural environment that encompasses them:

> . . . as much as any people of whom I have heard, the Navajos perceive and celebrate the beauty of the physical world.

There is a Navajo ceremonial song that celebrates the sounds that are made in the natural world, the particular voices that beautify the earth:

> Voice above,
> Voice of thunder,
> Speak from the
> dark of clouds;
> Voice below,
> Grasshopper voice,
> Speak from the
> green of plants;
> So may the earth
> be beautiful.

There is in the motion and meaning of this song a comprehension of the world that is peculiarly native, I believe, that is integral in the Native American mentality. Consider: The singer stands at the center of the natural world, at the source of its sound, of its motion, of its life. . . . At each level of his expression there is an extension of his awareness across the whole landscape. The voice above is the voice of thunder, and thunder rolls. Moreover, it issues from the impalpable dark clouds and runs upon their horizontal range. It is a sound that integrates the whole of the atmosphere. And even so, the voice below, that of the grasshopper, issues from the broad plain and multiplicity of plants. And of course the singer is mindful of much more than thunder and insects; we are given in his song the wide angle of his vision and his hearing—and we are given the testimony of his dignity, his trust, and his deep belief (1976:15–16).

The Navajo concept of *hózhǫ́* also encompasses social harmony. Within their families, kinship units, and larger social groups they seek harmony and avoid any show of aggressiveness, hostility, or self-assertiveness. They avoid impassioned confrontation at almost any cost. The ideal mode of all social relations is expressed in the term *k'é* which includes love, compassion, kindness, cooperativeness, friendliness, and peacefulness. Reichard notes that Navajo language does not have a word that signifies "love" as a separate or abstractable quality because love is subsumed under the general concepts of harmony (1950b:196). The Navajo word which is used most often by Navajos in translating the English term "love" is *ayóó'ó'óó'ní.* This term includes in its semantic canopy not only affection but respect, understanding, and, most importantly, trust. Navajos seem to believe that true or meaningful love cannot exist in isolation from understanding, sincere regard, and mutual trust. Reichard concluded the following:

These words illustrate a fundamental precept of the culture, the fostering and preservation of harmony from person to person, as well as from person to supernatural. The question is not how emotionally wrought up a person is in relation to another, but rather how his emotion is directed, how it works in practice, how much friction there is in social contacts. The degree of esteem is calculated in terms of harmony or the reverse; the terms express a social, rather than an individual viewpoint. It matches the preponderant aim of religion, to create and preserve harmony between man and all elements of the universe, among which man and all social groups are important units (1950b:199).

SUMMARY

In the pages above we can see how the value orientations and behavior patterns of the Navajo correlate with their basic metaphysical assumptions about the nature and operation of reality. I have generalized them as emphases upon creativity and control, order and beauty. In summarizing her interpretations of Navajo personality traits based on her analysis and interpretation of Navajo artwork, Hatcher concludes:

A summary of the interpretations which seem to apply include: need for achievement [this might better be stated as a need for expression], driving force and ardor, power in a controlled form, respect for individual autonomy, tension directed outward from the life space, harmony between individuals, emotions controlled by balance and moderation, warm emotions, a desire to analyze, to explore and adapt within limits, and a pervading emphasis on vitality and harmony and control. Perhaps equally significant is the absence of qualities which are interpreted to mean oppositional tendencies or ambiguity regarding social environment, feelings of isolation, suppressed emotions, and interpersonal conflict. The expression of anxiety is limited to a form which suggests relief from it, and aggressive forms appear only in some contexts, where they have the symbolic meaning of protection.

These interpretations seem entirely plausible when considered in terms of Navajo values and ideals, but as an expression of Navajo modal personality they do not fit very well with the accepted analyses in the literature (1974:214–15).

The accepted literature, mostly compiled during the Kluckhohn era of Harvard psychoanalytical research projects conducted mainly at Ramah, New Mexico, should, in my opinion, be transferred from the category "accepted" to the category of "questionable." Many of the culture and personality studies of this era have come under so much unfavorable scrutiny that the whole effort has been largely discounted by many anthropologists.

The Navajo emphases upon creativity and control, balance and beauty, actually reflect the basic complementary dualism of static and active. Control and balance (order) are essentially static oriented emphases, while creativity (activity) and beauty (harmony) are dynamic and active. Most of the other categories found in the Navajo conception of the constitution and operation of reality also divide into static and active domains. These include the word and the symbol, knowledge and language, and thought and speech. The sacred and secular domains of behavior are also divided into the static domain of the sacred, analogically associated with the male, and the active domain of the secular, analogically associated with the female. The synthesis of all these dualistic modes leads to the ideal of *hózhǫ́*.

The various pairs mentioned above and discussed in detail in earlier chapters are complementary. They are in the nature of things and are necessary for the full realization of *hózhǫ́*. Although they complement each other, Navajo culture does not give equal emphasis to both. Navajo culture definitely puts more emphasis on the active side, and that is what gives Navajo culture its dynamic quality.

A good example of this pattern of complementary but unequal pairing is found in the Navajo conception of the roles of males and females. During the episodes of the third underworld, the women decided they didn't need the men any more and offered to leave them. The men accepted the challenge and the sexes parted, each living separately on different sides of a river. Their experiment proved to be a failure and the women eventually decided that they could not live successfully without the men. This episode makes it clear that in Navajo conception the male and the female form a complementary and necessary pair. This does not, however, mean that they are exactly equal or equal in all things. The female, as the active, vital, creative, productive, and procreative being, is given more emphasis.

The Navajo view of reproduction or procreation is not exactly like the Western view of this process. In the West there is a tendency to think of the father and the mother as making an equal contribution to the procreation of a child. They are treated as equal parents and relatives on both sides are thought of as equal in their relationship to the child. The Navajo view is one in which the male provides the semen or seed necessary for conception but it is the mother who conceives the child in her womb, who nurtures it in her womb prenatally, who through pain and suffering gives it birth and even after birth it is the mother who primarily nurtures and sustains the life and well-being of the child. Although the father plays a necessary, important and complementary role in this process, it is not, in the Navajo view, equal to that of the mother.

In the active and free-flowing domain of weaving where the creation of new forms and designs is the rule, women also dominate in a realm that is normally a male activity in most cultures:

There are constants in the Navajo experience which underlie the tradition of these blankets. Foremost of these is a feeling of energy. . . .

The Navajos understand the world in terms of energy and change. They are a profoundly musical people whose ceremonies and rituals were sung; and for weaving of blankets there were specific chants for each phase of the process. . . .

. . . in most cultures textiles have been made by men who were part of a specific professional class. For the Navajo, weaving was not a separate profession—it was part of a woman's cycle of life. The Navajo culture is matriarchal and the blankets have a dynamic force and consistent aggressive quality which white culture has not considered a feminine trait (Berlant and Kahlenberg, 1972:45).

In the ceremonial domain where the emphasis is not on the generation of new life and forms but on the restoration of old states and forms through the performance of static, unchanging rites, the male takes a kind of appropriate priority. Although females play many important, necessary, and complementary roles in the performance of various rites, it would not be correct to say that these roles are equal to that played by men. This complementary inequality gives Navajo life its dynamic rhythm and harmony.

Just as perfect symmetry in art is basically static, perfect equality and balance between two parts of a pair also produces a static result. It is delicate imbalance and complementary inequality that give a dynamic relationship to paired elements. From my interpretation of Navajo art, I conclude that the Navajo aesthetic style is one of dynamic symmetry. From my analysis of Navajo world view, I conclude that the Navajo intellectual style is one of dynamic synthesis. I will elaborate briefly on each of these styles.

In art symmetry signifies the static and asymmetry the active:

> Symmetry signifies rest and binding, asymmetry motion and loosening, the one order and law, the other arbitrariness and accident, the one formal rigidity and constraint, the other life, play and freedom (Frey, 1952:16).

Both symmetry and asymmetry play a role in art and may have aesthetic appeal. The asymmetry which has the most aesthetic appeal is not the conjunction of two parts that are totally unalike and thus unrelated but the conjunction of similar and related parts that are, nevertheless, to some degree or in some way or ways contrasted to one another.

Artists and art interpreters make a distinction between static and dynamic symmetry:

> Static symmetry is the symmetry of inorganic form of 'even' units in the creation of form, of arithmetic ration: snowflakes, square grid buildings, city clocks. Dynamic symmetry is the symmetry of forms of growth—of growth of units of geometric ratio: shell forms, the dimensions of man, the forms of plants, hyperbolic (Markson, 1965:88).

Static symmetry derives from man's mental propensity towards simplicity and exact balance and man's emotional urge for unity, stability, and security. Dynamic symmetry derives from man's adventurous and creative nature, but its near symmetry suggests a pattern of controlled adventure and constrained creativity. Static symmetry is more characteristic of nonaesthetically based creations of man—buildings, houses, cities, retail goods, and so on.

Dynamic symmetry is more characteristic of the dynamic flow and flux found in nature and in the proportions of the human body and the growing plant.

Analysts and interpreters of Navajo art have disagreed as to whether symmetry is a dominant theme in Navajo art. Mills says it is not, while Barry says it is. Reichard says it is rare in sandpaintings but Hatcher says it is a dominant theme. The problem, as Hatcher notes (1974:74), is that different interpreters have different ideas as to what constitutes symmetry. Some see only mirror symmetry, perfectly balanced, as symmetry. Others see near symmetry and near balance as basically symmetrical. Hatcher argues that in European tradition the emphasis in symmetry is on balance, whereas in Navajo symmetry the emphasis is on repetition (1974:74–75). McAllester noted that repetition in Navajo music was dynamic because it contained a number of modes of variation such as interruption, alternation, return, pairing, progression, transection, and ambiguity (n.d.:12). Sandpaintings exhibit a similar kind of dynamic repetition:

The fact that for the Navajo it is repetition rather than balance that is the basic organizing principle is shown by the circumstance that the "same" painting may be laid out either in a rectangular format or in a circular one. In the first instance the arrangement is one of repetition, usually dynamic, and, while it is basically bilateral, the figures are not reversed, but "follow each other." The circular version of the painting consists of the same figure as in the rectangular one, with the field bent around to form a radial-rotation pattern. The latter form permits additional complexity by additions to both the radial and the rotational patterning. The possibilities of symmetry implicit in the idea of elements that can be repeated in a variety of relations to one another are far greater than the possibilities implied by opposition and balancing of two parts. The complexity and variation of repetition are perhaps the most characteristic feature of most Navajo drypaintings (Hatcher, 1974:74–75).

The slight but numerous variations found in basically symmetrical patterns is what gives Navajo symmetry its dynamic quality. In the analysis of the sandpainting in plate 7, it was noted that dynamic symmetry was expressed in the contrasts of diagonal lines and figures with horizontal lines and figures, in the use of pure colors against a neutral background, and in the alternation of colors in opposing figures. Apparently unfamiliar with the idea of dynamic symmetry, Hatcher sees these variations and contrasts in Navajo symmetry as rhythmical:

Rhythm in drypaintings takes the form of small variations in the repetition of the principal figures or design units. . . . A principal form of rhythmic variation is in color, with the main colors being varied or reversed in each figure. Other variations are in minor elements, such as in the shapes of objects and symbols accompanying each figure. There is rhythm, too, in the repetition of parallel lines and the intervals between them, which are varied in a repetitive way. In the more complex paintings, one could speak of multiple rhythms, since different patterns can be seen in the radial and rotational "movements" (1974:75–76).

Rhythm, of course, suggests movement and is opposed to the static quality of perfect symmetry and balance.

Dynamic symmetry is based on the idea of similar and complementary but inexact, imperfect, and unequal pairing or balancing. This is a dominant theme or pattern in the Navajo aesthetic style. It is not simple or static, but dynamic and active. It is binary and dualistic, but it is not opposed or mirror imagery. Although it often has an axis or axes, it is not split or fragmented. The total impact of Navajo works of art is a unity of diversity, a synthesis of differences, a harmony of divergence, and a confluence of contrast.

The Navajo intellectual style is one of dynamic synthesis. In their thinking and in their daily behavior Navajos are constantly and creatively integrating and synthesizing. The outward trappings of their whole culture seem to be made of creative syntheses of diverse customs from divergent cultures. This seems to derive from a compulsion to relate, order, and unify everything with which they come in contact or experience. Mills concludes:

> The fundamental pattern of the Navaho world view is dialectical: thesis, antithesis, synthesis. . . . Kierkegaard, I think, called anxiety the dizziness of freedom. For the Navaho, anxiety . . . is the dizziness of prospective synthesis which, raising life to the highest degree of power and control, is the consummation of the Navaho way. The synthetic symbols, however powerful, are far from static. The harmony that earth people attain is not a resolution of conflict but a transformation of unbearable tensions into bearable and constructive ones (1959:201–2).

The Navajo intellectual style is not content with the static nature of simple dualism. It reaches for the unity of creative synthesis. Of course, Navajo intellectuals recognize that unity can only be a function or an offspring of diversity. Diversity, however, does not need to be created but is inherent in the primordial condition of things. In this diversity they see a primary dualism of static and active. The generation of life and the creation of beauty involves the transformation of the static condition into the active form, but the bidirectional or cyclical nature of movement, life, and creation always returns movement to rest, life to death, and beauty to plainness. That is why life cannot be forever prolonged, movement cannot be forever perpetuated, order cannot be forever maintained, and beauty cannot be forever preserved. Thus life must be regenerated, movement rejuvenated, order restored, and beauty renewed and recreated. This never-ending process goes from static to active and from active to static. It is not surprising, then, that Changing Woman, the very essence and personification of regeneration, rejuvenation, renewal, and dynamic beauty, is the Supreme Mother of the Navajos and is the most blessed, the most revered, and the most benevolent of all the Holy People.

And, appropriately, she is the child of the static male *Są'ah Naagháii* and the active female *Bik'eh Hózhǫ́*. This, I believe, is the model of creative synthesis that underlies and pervades all of Navajo culture, and its predominance in Navajo language and art has been the topic and focus of this book.

We Navajos
are always learning,
it is our way,
it is our eternal transformation
like a seed.
We are seeds,
and we plant ourselves.

This poem was written about R. C. Gorman, the famous Navajo artist, by Jim McGrath (PBS film, "R. C. Gorman," 1976).

Notes

INTRODUCTION

1. I did do a sociological survey of the Rough Rock/Black Mountain area during the summer of 1969.

CHAPTER 1

1. It has become customary for scholars to translate *Diyin Dine'é* as "Holy People," and to avoid confusion I follow this practice. However, I think this translation is incorrect because it gives the connotation of being infinitely good, perfect, and worthy of homage, which is far from the Navajo conception of these beings.

2. Robert Young doubts this etymology and considers it to be an inaccurate folk etymology.

3. Nearly all people are part good and part evil (motivated in part toward good and harmony and in part toward evil and chaos). When one dies, the evil remains behind with the physical body and thus it must be avoided (Robert Young, personal communication).

4. I calculated this number by multiplying all the possible verbal prefixes and combinations of verbal prefixes times all possible conjugations of person, number, tense, mode, and aspect of the verbs "to go (by walking)" and "to go (by running)."

5. Actually this prefix should be written as *ho* in contrast to *ni* with the rule of "*ni*-absorption" giving the high tone *hó*.

CHAPTER 3

1. These terms are appropriate only where the nouns are used predicatively; for example, *níléidi daakǫ'* 'over there, there are probably many fires'. These terms are not used as subjects or objects of verbs.

2. Under blue I am including what English speakers call green as well as blue. Navajos do not normally distinguish between what English speakers call blue and what English speakers call green.

CHAPTER 4

1. In contrast, among the Pueblos, weaving is primarily a male activity.

2. Although aniline dyes are now available to Navajo weavers and they are frequently used, many of the best weavers still prefer to use only natural dyes.

205

Bibliography

Aberle, David F.
  1961. The Navaho. In *Matrilineal Kinship,* ed. David M. Schneider and Kathleen Gough, pp. 96–201. Berkeley: University of California Press.
  1963. Some Sources of Flexibility in Navajo Social Organization. *Southwestern Journal of Anthropology* 19:1–18.

Astrov, Margaret
  1950. The Concept of Motion as the Psychological Leitmotif of Navaho Life and Literature. *Journal of American Folklore* 63: 45–56.

Austin, J. L.
  1962. *How to Do Things with Words.* Oxford: Clarendon Press.

Bahti, Tom
  1970. *Southwestern Indian Ceremonials.* Las Vegas, Nev.: K.C. Publications.

Berger, Peter, and Luckmann, Thomas
  1966. *The Social Construction of Reality.* Garden City, N.Y.: Doubleday and Co.

Berlant, Anthony, and Kahlenberg, Mary
  1972. Blanket Statements. *Art News* 71 (Summer): 42–71.

Busignani, Alberto
  1971. *Pollock.* Feltham, Middlesex: The Hamlyn Publishing Group, Ltd.

Chaitin, Gregory J.
  1975. Randomness and Mathematical Proof. *Scientific American* 232 (5): 47–53.

Creamer, Mary Helen
  1974. Ranking in Navajo Nouns. *Diné Bizaad Náníl'íjh*; *Navajo Language Review* 1(1): 29–38.

Downs, James F.
  1964. *Animal Husbandry in Navajo Society and Culture.* Berkeley: University of California Press.

D'Udine, Jean [A. Cozanet]
  1910. *L'art et le gueste.* Paris.

Eliade, Mircea
  1959. *The Sacred and the Profane.* New York: Harcourt, Brace and World, Inc.

Fishler, Stanley
  1953. *In the Beginning; A Navaho Creation Myth.* Utah University Anthropological Paper No. 13.

Freed, Stanley A., and Freed, Ruth S.
  1970. A Note on Regional Variation in Navajo Kinship Terminology. *American Anthropologist,* 72: 1439–44.

Frey, Dagobert
    1952. On the Problem of Symmetry in Art. In *Symmetry,* ed. Hermann
        Weyl. Princeton, N.J.: Princeton University Press.
Gearing, Frederick O.
    1970. *The Face of the Fox.* Chicago: Aldine Publishing Co.
Geertz, Clifford
    1966. Religion as a Cultural System. In *Anthropological Approaches to the
        Study of Religion,* ed. Michael Banton. New York: Frederick A.
        Praeger.
    1973. *The Interpretation of Cultures.* New York: Basic Books.
Goddard, Pliny Earle
    1933. Navajo Texts. *Anthropological Papers of the American Museum of
        Natural History* 34: 1–179. New York: The American Museum of
        Natural History.
Haile, Berard
    1943. Soul Concepts of the Navaho. *Annali Lateranensi* 7: 59–94.
    1949. *Emergence Myth According to the Hanelthnayhe or Upward-Reaching
        Rite.* Rewritten by M. C. Wheelwright. Navajo Religion Series 3.
        Sante Fe: Museum of Navajo Ceremonial Art.
Hale, Kenneth
    1973. A Note on Subject-Object Inversion in Navajo. In *Issues in Lin-
        guistics; Papers in Honor of Henry and Renée Kahane,* ed. Braj B.
        Kachru et al., pp. 300–309. Urbana: University of Illinois Press.
Hatcher, Evelyn Payne
    1974. *Visual Metaphors: A Formal Analysis of Navajo Art.* The American
        Ethnological Society Monograph 58. St. Paul: West Publishing
        Co.
Hoijer, Harry
    1945. Classificatory Verb Stems in Apachean Languages. *International
        Journal of American Linguistics* 11: 13–23.
    1964. Cultural Implications of Some Navaho Linguistic Categories. In
        Language in Culture and Society, ed. Dell Hymes, pp. 143–53. New
        York: Harper and Row, Publishers.
Humboldt, Wilhelm von
    1971. *Linguistic Variability and Intellectual Development.* (Originally pub-
        lished in Berlin, 1836.) Coral Gables: University of Miami Press.
Kahlenberg, Mary H., and Berlant, Anthony
    1972. *The Navajo Blanket.* New York: Frederick A. Praeger.
Kinget, G. Marian
    1952. *The Drawing-Completion Test.* New York: Grune and Stratton, Inc.
Kluckhohn, Clyde K.
    1949. The Philosophy of the Navaho Indians. In *Ideological Differences
        and World Order,* ed. F. S. C. Northrop, pp. 356–84. New Haven:
        Yale University Press.

Ladd, John
1957. *The Structure of a Moral Code.* Cambridge: Harvard University Press.
Lamphere, Louise
1969. Symbolic Elements in Navajo Ritual. *Southwestern Journal of Anthropology* 25: 279–305.
Landar, Herbert J.
1962. Fluctuation of Forms in Navaho Kinship Terminology. *American Anthropologist* 64: 985–1000.
Langer, Suzanne
1957. *Philosophy in a New Key.* 3d ed. Cambridge: Harvard University Press.
Markson, Morley
1965. Symmetry, Design Operation, and the Soul. In *Design and Planning,* ed. Martin Krampen. New York: Hastings House.
Matthews, Washington
1902. The Night Chant. *Memoirs of the American Museum of Natural History* 6. New York: The American Museum of Natural History.
McAllester, David
n.d.   The First Snake Song. Unpublished manuscript.
Mills, George Thompson
1959. *Navaho Art and Culture.* Colorado Springs: Taylor Museum of Colorado Springs, Fine Arts Center.
Momaday, N. Scott
1976. A First American Views His Land. *National Geographic* July: 13–18.
O'Bryan, Aileen
1956. *The Dine: Origin Myths of the Navaho Indians.* U. S. Bureau of American Ethnology Bulletin 163. Washington, D. C.: The Smithsonian Institution.
Piaget, Jean
1970. *Structuralism.* New York: Basic Books.
Rappaport, Roy A.
1974. Obvious Aspects of Ritual. *Cambridge Anthropology* 2: 2–60.
Reichard, Gladys A.
1939. *Navajo Medicine Man.* New York: J. J. Augustin.
1943. Human Nature as Conceived by the Navajo Indians. *Review of Religion* May: 343–60.
1944. *Prayer: The Compulsive Word.* American Ethnological Society Monograph 7. Seattle: University of Washington Press.
1949. The Character of the Navaho Verb Stem. *Word* 5: 55–76.
1950a.*Navaho Religion: A Study of Symbolism.* New York: Bollingen Foundation.
1950b.Language and Cultural Pattern. *American Anthropologist* 52: 194–206.

1951. *Navajo Grammar.* American Ethnological Society Publication 21. New York: J. J. Augustin.

1968. *Navajo Shepherd and Weaver.* Glorieta, N.M.: Rio Grande Press.

Ritchie, A. D.

1936. *The Natural History of the Mind.* London: Longmans, Green and Co.

Sapir, Edward, and Hoijer, Harry

1963. The Phonology and Morphology of the Navaho Language. *Linguistics* 50. University of California Publications.

Shepardson, Mary, and Hammond, Blodwen

1970. *The Navajo Mountain Community.* Berkeley: University of California Press.

Stevenson, James

1886. Ceremonial of Hasjelfi Dailjis. *Annual Report of the Bureau of American Ethnology* 8: 229–85.

Werner, Oswald, and Begishe, Kenneth

1968. Styles of Learning: The Evidence from Navajo. Unpublished manuscript.

Wheelwright, Mary C.

1942. *Navajo Creation Myth.* Navajo Religion Series 1. Sante Fe: Museum of Navajo Ceremonial Art.

Witherspoon, Gary

1970. A New Look at Navajo Social Organization. *American Anthropologist* 73: 55–65.

1971. Navajo Categories of Objects at Rest. *American Anthropologist* 73: 110–27.

1974. The Central Concepts of Navajo World View (I). *Linguistics* 119(January):41–59.

1975a.*Navajo Kinship and Marriage.* Chicago: University of Chicago Press.

1975b.The Central Concepts of Navajo World View (II). *Linguistics* 161:69–88.

Wyman, Leland C.

1970. *Blessingway.* Tucson: University of Arizona Press.

Young, Robert W., and Morgan, William

1943. *The Navaho Language.* Phoenix: Educational Division, Bureau of Indian Affairs.

1951. *A Vocabulary of Colloquial Navaho.* Phoenix: United States Indian Service.

Index

Please remember that this is a library book,
and that it belongs only temporarily to each
person who uses it. Be considerate. Do
not write in this, or any, library book.